A TEACHER'S GUIDE TO
Getting Started WITH
BEGINNING
WRITERS

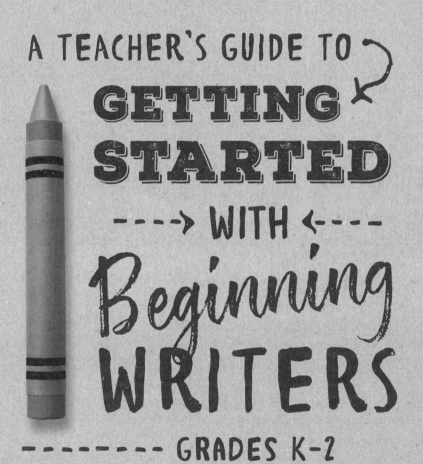

A TEACHER'S GUIDE TO GETTING STARTED WITH Beginning WRITERS

GRADES K-2

KATIE WOOD RAY *with* **LISA CLEAVELAND**

Heinemann | Portsmouth, NH

Heinemann
361 Hanover Street
Portsmouth, NH 03801–3912
www.heinemann.com

Offices and agents throughout the world

> *The authors have dedicated a great deal of time and effort to writing the content of this book, and their written expression is protected by copyright law. We respectfully ask that you do not adapt, reuse, or copy anything on third-party (whether for-profit or not-for-profit) lesson-sharing websites. As always, we're happy to answer any questions you may have.*
> —Heinemann Publishers

"Dedicated to Teachers" is a trademark of Greenwood Publishing Group, Inc.

The authors and publisher wish to thank those who have generously given permission to reprint borrowed material:

Alphabet Teaching Chart by Steps to Literacy, www.stepstoliteracy.com. Copyright © 1998 by Steps to Literacy. Reprinted with permission from the copyright holder.

Interior photographs: page 3, © Erik Isakson / Getty Images; page 7, © Caiaimage / Paul Bradbury / Getty Images; page 42, © Wavebreak Media / Shutterstock; page 64, © Hero Images / Getty Images; page 97, © Blend Images—Kidstock / Getty Images; page 97, © Kidstock / Getty Images; page 113, © FatCamera / Getty Images / HIP

Library of Congress Cataloging-in-Publication Data
Names: Ray, Katie Wood, author. | Cleaveland, Lisa B., author.
Title: A teacher's guide to getting started with beginning writers / Katie Wood Ray with Lisa Cleaveland.
Description: Portsmouth, NH : Heinemann, [2018] | Series: The classroom essentials series
Identifiers: LCCN 2018015476 | ISBN 9780325099149
Subjects: LCSH: English language—Composition and exercises—Study and teaching (Elementary) | Language arts (Elementary) | Writers' workshops.
Classification: LCC LB1576 .R3736 2018 | DDC 372.62/3—dc23

LC record available at https://lccn.loc.gov/2018015476

Editor: Zoë Ryder White
Production: Hilary Goff
Cover and interior designs, typesetting: Vita Lane
Manufacturing: Steve Bernier

Printed in the United States of America on acid-free paper
22 21 20 19   VP   2 3 4 5

This book is dedicated to teachers everywhere
who have unshakable faith in the remarkable
capabilities of beginning writers.

Book MAP

Welcome

A PLACE FOR CHILDREN TO MAKE ←---- BOOKS 1

WHY MAKE BOOKS? 2

WHAT WRITERS NEED
TO GET STARTED 2

    Time 3
    Space 3
    Blank books 4
    Writing tools 4
    An image of bookmaking 4

LEARNING *THROUGH* LANGUAGE,
LEARNING *ABOUT* LANGUAGE 5

BELIEFS GUIDE ACTIONS 6

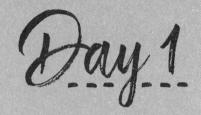

Day 1

INVITE CHILDREN TO GET STARTED 8

HELPING CHILDREN UNDERSTAND
TIME THAT'S GOVERNED
BY PURPOSE 10

THE DIFFERENCE BETWEEN
WRITING AS PROCESS
AND WRITING AS PROCEDURE 10

QUESTIONS TO HELP CHILDREN
THINK ABOUT PEOPLE WHO
MAKE BOOKS 11

PICTURING WRITERS AT WORK 12–14

PLANTING SEEDS OF TEACHING
AS YOU SHARE CHILDREN'S
FINISHED BOOKS   16–18

DECIDING WHO WILL SHARE AT THE
END OF WRITING WORKSHOP   23–24

TELLING STORIES OF PROCESS   25

BIG IDEAS AND
TEACHING POSSIBILITIES   26

Day 2

NAME CHILDREN'S ACTIONS AS PROCESS   28

QUESTIONS THAT BELIEVE CHILDREN
INTO BEING   30–32

UNDERSTANDING WHAT IT MEANS TO
BE FINISHED   33

THREE KEY READING STRATEGIES FOR
BEGINNING WRITERS   37

VALUING CHILDREN'S LONG, SLOW WORK
ON A BOOK   39

RECOGNIZING CHILDREN'S ACTIONS AS
WRITING PROCESS   40

BIG IDEAS AND TEACHING POSSIBILITIES   41

Day 3 SET EXPECTATIONS FOR PICTURES AND WORDS 42

POSITIONING CHILDREN SO THEY'RE WILLING TO TRY WRITING WORDS 44

NARRATING YOUR ACTIONS TO SHOW CHILDREN HOW WRITTEN LANGUAGE WORKS 46

COMPOSING WITH WORDS INVOLVES A LOT MORE THAN JUST SPELLING 47

EMBEDDING TEACHING POINTS IN YOUR AUTHENTIC TALK WITH CHILDREN 48

    Embedding big ideas about texts 49

    Embedding big ideas about process 50

    Embedding big ideas about what it means to be a writer 51

RESISTING THE URGE TO OVERTEACH 52–53

MAINTAINING CHILDREN'S CONFIDENCE ONCE THEY START WRITING WORDS 58–59

A PROBLEM WITH DICTATION 60

BIG IDEAS AND TEACHING POSSIBILITIES 61

Day 4 OFFER CHILDREN STRATEGIES FOR WORD MAKING 64

THE TYPICAL RANGE OF WORD-MAKING DEVELOPMENT 65

EXPANDING THE DEFINITION OF READING (TO MAKE SENSE OF BEGINNING WRITING) 66–67

THE USEFULNESS OF ALPHABET CHARTS 70

STRATEGIES FOR WORD MAKING 72–73

THE IMPORTANCE OF NOTICING AND NAMING—AND *WHAT* TO NOTICE 75

WHY YOUNG CHILDREN NEED TO TALK DURING WRITING WORKSHOP 76

EDITING POSSIBILITIES FOR BEGINNING WRITERS 78–79

BIG IDEAS AND TEACHING POSSIBILITIES 80

Day 5

SHOW CHILDREN HOW TO MANAGE BOOK MAKING OVER TIME 82

WHAT HAPPENS WHEN WRITERS REREAD? 84

PICTURES FIRST OR WORDS FIRST? 84

DECIDING WHEN A BOOK IS FINISHED 86

TEACHING CHILDREN TO READ THEIR BOOKS 88

LEARNING ABOUT THE WRITING PROCESS IN THE CONTEXT OF ILLUSTRATIONS 91

TYPICAL DEVELOPMENT AS CHILDREN LEARN TO KEEP THEIR MEANINGS CONSISTENT 92

BIG IDEAS AND TEACHING POSSIBILITIES 93

Days After

SUPPORT CHILDREN IN THE EARLY WEEKS OF SCHOOL 98

SHARING FINISHED BOOKS 99

ENCOURAGING FEARLESS SPELLING 101

EMBRACING DIFFERENT WRITERS' PROCESSES 103

ILLUSTRATING WITH INTENTION 105

MANAGING ONGOING WORK 110

CELEBRATING GROWTH OVER TIME 111

WHEN THE CAMERA SHUTS OFF... 113

BOOKSHELF AND OTHER CITATIONS 114

About the Videos in This Book

The online videos connected to *A Teacher's Guide to Getting Started with Beginning Writers* document a group of children in the first five days of school as their teacher establishes a daily routine of bookmaking in writing workshop, and then captures some critical moments in the early weeks after those first days. Each day is segmented into short clips indicated by this icon , and the text that follows each clip builds important understandings about working with beginning writers that spin out of the teaching you've seen. At times, you will see both of us working with children: Lisa as the classroom teacher and Katie as a participant researcher.

Our hope is that the video helps you picture doing this work with your own students—whether it's the beginning of the year or sometime later, whether you teach in a rural mountain school like this one or in a busy city or anywhere in between. As Donald Graves taught us, children *want* to write. We hope this book builds your confidence to let them write—even the beginners. *Especially* the beginners.

To access the online videos, visit
http://hein.pub/Classroom Essentials-login.
**Enter your email address and password
(or click "Create New Account" to set up
an account). Once you have logged in, enter
keycode** CEBEGWRIT **and click "Register."**

Welcome

A PLACE FOR
CHILDREN
TO MAKE ←----
BOOKS

For more than twenty-five years, the children in Lisa Cleaveland's kindergarten and first-grade classes have started making their own books on the first full day of school. By the third week or so, bookmaking is a daily routine and the children work with an independence that sometimes seems extraordinary for writers and illustrators so young. If you were to visit Lisa's classroom later in February or May, you would see the children growing and changing as writers as they study craft and genre and process in units of study across the year. But nothing is as critical as the first few weeks of school when the routine of making books is established and the tone is set for the entire year.

How does she do it, year after year? How does Lisa help five- and six-year-olds believe they are writers and illustrators capable of making books? How does she help them become so willing to take risks and try things that are new and challenging? How does she help them engage with the process of writing and all the thinking and decision-making that accompanies it? How does she initiate children into the "shop talk" of writers, using new words to represent new ideas about all this new work? What informs her teaching in those critical first days and weeks when children are just getting started with writing? This Classroom Essentials book came about as a way to answer these questions.

In video and in words, *Getting Started with Beginning Writers* tells the story of a group of children and their teacher embarking on a year of study together in a writing workshop. As the story unfolds, alongside it you will find all kinds of ideas, information, strategies, and tips. If you are a new teacher (or are new to writing workshop), this book will show you in clear and simple terms what to do to establish a routine for writing in your classroom. If you're an experienced workshop teacher, the book will help you imagine new possibilities for getting started. If you've ever longed for beginning writers to show more independence during units of study across the year, then this book is for you.

BOOKSHELF

LANGUAGE STORIES AND LITERACY LESSONS
Jerry Harste, Virginia Woodward, and Carolyn Burke

EMERGING LITERACY
Dorothy Strickland and Lesley Mandel Morrow, eds.

The researchers in these two classic texts shine a light on the critical role approximation plays in the development of beginning writers and readers. Their names read like a "Who's Who" in early emergent literacy research, including also Teale, Sulzby, Glazer, Cullinan, Schickendans, Taylor, and more.

First Things First: The Practice

Before we start our story, there are a few things you need to know about the practice you will see. First, and most importantly, the *work* part of writing *work*shop is making books. If you ask the children what they do in writing workshop, they'll say, "We make books." To help you imagine what that means, here's a snapshot of children doing just that in April. Like the children in our story, these children also started making books way back in August on their very first day of school.

A Snapshot of Writing Workshop in April

Making books:

is developmentally appropriate. Young children love to make things and they bring an easy sense of play to *making*.

encourages children to do bigger work and develop stamina for writing.

causes children to live like writers when they're away from their desks as they think about their books in progress.

makes the "reading like writers" connection so clear.

helps children begin to understand the process of composition and decision-making.

helps children begin to understand genre, purpose, and audience.

Watch closely and you will see how each of these reasons to make books is clear even in the first five days of writing workshop.

What children need to get started making books is very simple. They need time, space, blank books, writing tools, and an image of bookmaking.

TIME

Extending the time for independent work a little each day, Lisa eventually devotes a full hour to the routines of writing workshop.

 10–20 minutes
Writers' meeting (whole class): the teacher leads conversations, demonstrations, and inquiries connected to a unit of study.

30–40 minutes
Independent work: the children make books.

 5–10 minutes
Share and reflection (whole class): writers tell stories of process.

An hour may seem like a lot of time, but when you consider that children are also growing as readers as they write, it seems a wise investment. If you devote less time to your writing workshop, you'll still need to allocate the appropriate *proportion* of time for teaching, writing, and sharing.

SPACE

When it's time to make books, the children spread out around the room and choose where they want to work. There are tables for children who want to sit in groups, a few individual desks for those who want to work alone, and lapboards for those who want to sit on the floor. Deciding where you can do your best work as a writer is one of the decisions Lisa wants the children to own, so she offers guidance and support for it as needed across the year.

BLANK BOOKS

Lisa starts the year with pre-stapled books of five to six blank pages each; she uses plain white paper (no lines) in landscape orientation. Lines set an expectation for print that makes some children think, "I know what's supposed to go on those lines and I don't know how to do that, so I *can't*." And we don't want *can't*, of course. Blank paper is just more invitational. Later in the kindergarten year, or at the beginning of first or second grade, you might offer children a choice of books made with paper with some lines for writing and some space for pictures, like this:

WRITING TOOLS

Lisa keeps the tools for bookmaking simple. She has separate tubs for crayons, colored pencils, and markers. Children decide which medium they want to use and pick a tub up on their way out to work. Laminated alphabet charts are available for those who need them, and hanging file folders hold the children's books, both finished and in progress, at the end of each day's workshop. Another bin holds the pre-stapled blank books children can get when they're ready to start something new. That's it!

AN IMAGE OF BOOKMAKING

For children to make books, they first need to know what books look like, which most do, and they need to know that *people* make books—they don't just come from the store or the library. These may seem like pretty obvious ideas, but if children don't understand that a finished book is the end result of someone's work to make that book, then it's hard for them to see themselves doing that work. Lisa also shows her students photographs of children *engaged* in bookmaking, taking the actions that lead from ideas to finished books.

Page from a book with lines

Page from a book without lines

LEARNING *THROUGH* LANGUAGE, LEARNING *ABOUT* LANGUAGE

In writing workshop, most of the teaching is about the process and craft of bookmaking, and children learn *through* language as they use what they know about writing to help them make books. But research shows children also need to learn *about* language, and much of this teaching happens outside the writing workshop where Lisa plans for daily, direct instruction about language—the alphabet, phonological awareness, spelling and word patterns, sentence construction, conventions, and so on. This teaching is both systematic and responsive to ongoing assessment of what children need. In the background of video in the "Days After" chapter of this book, you can see tracks of this teaching on the whiteboard at the front of the meeting area.

In many primary classrooms, children spend most of their time learning *about* language and not so much time learning *through* language. Why is it important to have both? Well, choose your metaphor. Imagine trying to learn to

- **play basketball by doing drills (but never playing in a game).**
- **knit by watching a video (but never trying your hand at a scarf).**
- **cook by reading recipes (but never going into the kitchen).**

Of course you can't imagine this! Anyone learning to do anything needs to learn both by finding out about it and by doing it.

Next Things Next: The Beliefs

If the practical side of the workshop seems simple, that's because it is! In fact, for years when people have asked us, "How do you get them started?" we've answered, "Well, it's not rocket science." As you watch Lisa teach in these first five days, we hope that you feel the easy nature of her teaching and that it doesn't seem out of reach to you in a rocket-science kind of way. But just remember, Lisa's teaching has an easy feel to it not because it's easy, but because she is at ease with the beliefs guiding her actions.

In the teaching you will see, Lisa's beliefs about what she is doing will surface again and again—in her plans, her actions, her responses. After five days, it will no doubt be clear that Lisa believes

- Writing must be a predictable, daily *routine*.
- Children need to see themselves as writers, each with a unique *identity*.
- Writing is a process of *decision-making* and *action*.
- Writers need a disposition for *risk-taking*.
- Writers need a sense of *momentum* to know they are growing.
- Writers work with a sense of *craft* guiding them, and they learn craft from *mentors*.
- Teachers must *act as if* children are capable, competent writers.

Let's Get Started

Our hope is that this book will offer you vision, insight, and practical support for how to start a writing workshop with beginning writers. Here's what you'll find.

VISION

Divided into short segments, this book allows you to read the story of teaching and then watch video of all the whole-class teaching from the first five days of school, along with seven bonus clips that showcase important teaching during the first few weeks.

INSIGHT

After each video segment, a "Now Consider" section explores key ideas related to the teaching you've seen. These ideas will help you build the knowledge base you need to launch your own writing workshop and support beginning writers as they get started making their own books.

PRACTICAL SUPPORT

At the end of each day's teaching, you'll find an "In Your Own Classroom" section to help you plan your work with beginning writers. *Getting Started with Beginning Writers* is not a script you can follow, of course, because so much of Lisa's teaching is in response to what her students say and do. But regardless of the children sitting in front of you, and regardless of whether it's the beginning of the school year or sometime later, there are very specific big ideas that need to be communicated in the first days of writing workshop and practical ways to help children understand them. This book will show you the way to those big ideas.

SO ONCE AGAIN, WELCOME!

Day 1

INVITE CHILDREN TO GET STARTED

Lisa has had a lot of first days of writing workshop. And while every one of them has been a little bit different, over time she's learned what's most important about helping beginning writers get started. Your classroom and your students will be different too, but Lisa's experience can help you plan a first day with what matters most in mind.

At Lisa's school, kindergarten classes start the year with a staggered entry. Ten children attend the first full day, five more join them the next day, and the remaining children the next. The staggered entry helps those who are experiencing school for the first time make the transition more easily.

Day 1:
The Writers' Meeting Begins

On the first day, ten children have been playing and exploring in centers (sand, science, water table, painting, housekeeping, Legos, blocks) for a while when Lisa has them clean up and join her on the carpet for their first writers' meeting of the year. In the opening moments of the meeting, Lisa explains what writing workshop is and then invites children to think about the bookmaking they will soon do.

Day 1, Part 1

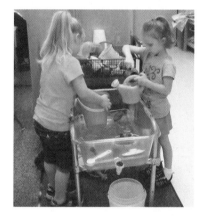

NOW CONSIDER

Writing workshop will be *a time* every day when children make books. Lisa helps children understand the workshop as *a time* by connecting it to other, familiar times that are governed by a purpose. Imagine the connections you could make:

CENTER TIME
is when you choose
a center to go to and
you play and explore.

LUNCHTIME
is when you eat so you're
not hungry anymore.

RECESS
is when you go outside
to run around and let
some energy out.

DISMISSAL
is when you line up
as walkers, car riders, and
bus riders to go home.

BATH TIME
is when you take a bath.

BEDTIME
is when you go to sleep.

WRITING WORKSHOP
is when you make books.

"How do you make books?"

Of course, this is a logical question (and a child asks Lisa this almost immediately!), but it's not a question you should answer. If you give students directions for how to make books ("First you do this, then you do this, and don't forget this . . ."), you turn the workshop into a procedure—a task to be completed. Children will expect you to direct their work and will wait for you to tell them what to do next. Too many workshops get off to shaky starts (and sometimes never recover) because teachers give too many directions for how to go about the work of the workshop.

Writing workshop is a time when children make books, but it's also a time when children *figure out how* to make books. And the *figuring out how* part is way more important than the making part. This is why Lisa never answers the child's question about how to make a book. Instead, she invites her students to think about how it is that they might go from a completely blank book to a completely finished book all on their own. "What do you think you'll need?" she asks them.

Imagine picking up a book in your room. Let's say it's a Kevin Henkes book. With your students, think about how that book was made.

- Who made this book? What is this person's name? What does he look like?
- What tools do you think he used?
- How do you think he did it? Did he draw the pictures first? Write the words first?
- How long do you think it took him?
- Would *you* like to make a book?

Thinking about the person who made a book is an important first step toward mentorship. Children need to see themselves as being *like* the people who make books—so make those people real.

Tip

At the beginning of the year, share books where the same person is both author and illustrator. This matches the work your students will do to make books.

Because some children believe they don't know how to write, the verb *make* is more inclusive and inviting.

DICTIONARY ◄- - - -

MAKE

māk/ | *verb*

1. form (something) by putting parts together or combining substances; construct; create. *"my grandmother made a dress for me"*
synonyms: construct, build, assemble, put together, manufacture, produce, fabricate, create, form, fashion, model. *"he makes models"*

2. cause (something) to exist or come about; bring about. *"the drips had made a pool on the floor"*

You may have children who doubt whether they can do this whole bookmaking thing. This is the time to *act as if*, just as Lisa does when Heidi says, "I don't know how to." Lisa responds, "Well, you'll get started knowing how," and then she just keeps right on going. Children sometimes think you expect them to do things they don't know how to do, but once you call *whatever* they do with pencils and markers in hand *making books*, they'll believe they can do it. You just have to get them out there that first time. And remember, most children will do *something* if they have paper and markers in hand, and most others will follow along eventually.

BOOKSHELF

FROM COMMUNICATION TO CURRICULUM
Douglas Barnes

CLASSROOM DISCOURSE
Courtney B. Cazden

These language theorists help us understand how much the words of our teaching—like the difference between *make* and *write*—matter.

Day 1:
The Writers' Meeting Continues

As the meeting continues, Lisa shows the children a chart with photos depicting workshop routines. Her students recognize many of the children from last year's class in the photos—some of them are even siblings! Lisa's goal is not to establish the routines on the chart on this first day. The chart simply shows the kinds of things writers do during workshop so the children can better imagine themselves doing these same things.

Each year, Lisa creates a new "workshop routines" chart with her class in the early weeks of school. They take lots of pictures, and then talk together about which photos best capture each routine and should go on the chart, and what language they should use for the labels. Every year the chart is a little different, and the process of making it together helps children understand the routines in important ways.

▶ **Day 1, Part 2**

Writing Workshop Routines

· Wait in line nicely to get the book you are working on.
· Get the tools you need: markers, colored pencils, crayons, pencils, alphabet cards...
· Find a good place in the

class to write.
· A place that you can focus.
· <u>Always</u> re-read your book!

· Sometimes writers need time to think...
· Find your best way to get illustrations and text in your book.
· If you think your book is finished check the "Is My Book Finished Chart."

And... read it to a friend!
· If your book is finished... Start a new one!
· Make sure your new book is opening the correct way!

· Give it a date stamp.
· Always write until the bell rings (then you have 5 more minutes).
· Put the book you are working on in the <u>front</u> of your writing folder.
· Get ready for "the share."

NOW CONSIDER

The old saying "a picture is worth a thousand words" certainly holds true in this case. Photographs of children engaged in writing workshop send a clear message: *If they can do it, so can you!* How you talk about the photos is also important. You build understandings with what you say and how you say it. Think about the kinds of things Lisa says and the messages she sends with her words.

"They went, and they got pencils or colored pencils or markers . . . Then they took them to a table where they were going to work."

Language like this helps children think about engaging with the tools and doing the *work* of writing *work*shop.

"Gosh, you'll start a book today, but I guarantee you won't finish it today, because books take a long time to make."

To help children develop stamina, encourage long work on books right from the start.

"Look at this guy . . . He's kind of working in the floor. He felt like he could do his best writing on the floor. So I'm going to let you choose where you're going to work in the room."

Progressive verbs like *working* suggest process in a deliberate way. Children make decisions based on what will help them do their best writing.

"And these guys seem to work really well together and they're helping each other out."

Writing workshop is a place where we will work together.

"This girl has written this whole book, and she's pointing to her words and reading back what she's done. You'll be doing that."

Be sure to talk often and with confidence about a future that includes all kinds of things children aren't doing *yet*.

"She had lots of cats at her house and she wrote about cats all the time."

As soon as you know things about your students as writers, use comments like this to powerfully reinforce their writing identities.

"You're going to go out and write and work on your book until this timer buzzes."

Writers are finished when the time is up, not when their books are finished.

Tip

Helping students picture writers at work will be a challenge if you don't have any photos of children making books, so feel free to show your students the photos in this book just to get them started. Then, have your camera ready that very first day and start documenting your own writers at work.

Sharing photos of writers at work doesn't answer the question "How do you make books?" Photos help children imagine what it looks like when writers—like them—make books. To make a space for yourself to teach, you need students to become fiercely independent, and independence begins with children finding their own processes for making books. Whenever you doubt their ability to figure out how, just remember that they can't go from a blank book to a finished book without *some* sort of process. If you can just get them started, you can look closely at what they're doing and help them do it a little bit better each day. But independence first!

> **Independence begins with children finding their own processes for making books.**

BOOKSHELF

JOINING THE LITERACY CLUB
Frank Smith

The "literacy club" is one of the most important metaphors for describing the social nature of literacy learning. Think about how photographs of students participating in writing workshop help children literally *see* the club they are joining.

Day 1:
The Writers' Meeting Concludes

In the final part of the meeting, Lisa quickly shows the children some books written by other kindergarteners, and then she takes time to read one of them. Lisa hopes these books will help children think about topics they might write and draw about in their books, but she also hopes they'll make children think, "Hey, that looks like something I can do!"

Day 1, Part 3

NOW CONSIDER

You can support your students in so many important ways when you're intentional about *how* you read aloud from children's work. Lisa reads the book *Roller Skating* so it sounds like a very good book. Her intonation, articulation, and gestures honor the child's book as a *real* book worthy of her best read-aloud voice. She shows she clearly values children's writing in the same way she values the writing of professional writers.

Lisa also plants little seeds of teaching all across the reading:

①

Cover:
Roller Skating

WHAT LISA SAYS

"This is a book that a kindergartner wrote, just like you. *Roller Skating*. It's by Logan. And look, he's got that picture on the front and his words and his name. I want to make sure everybody puts their names on the front today."

TEACHING SEEDS

When you say "just like you," it helps children see themselves as capable bookmakers.

Point out the parts of a book you want children to include.

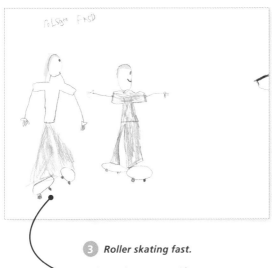

(2) *Roller skating is fun.*

WHAT LISA SAYS

"And this is looking at people's heads. These are the tops of their heads as they're skating around."

TEACHING SEEDS

Model how to read like a writer, and draw attention to interesting decisions the child has made.

(3) *Roller skating fast.*

WHAT LISA SAYS

"And it's apparently so fast that this was somebody—they've skated off the page they're so fast! Look at the wheels on the skates."

TEACHING SEEDS

The idea that pictures have meaning is critical as students learn to compose with illustrations as well as words.

(4) *Roller skating is cool.*

WHAT LISA SAYS

"Look at this (pointing at the motion lines). What do you think that is?"

TEACHING SEEDS

Invite children to engage in reading like writers with you.

5 *Roller skating is awesome.*

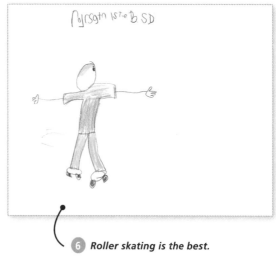

6 *Roller skating is the best.*

7 *Hi, My name is Logan and I am the illustrator and author of Roller Skating*

WHAT LISA SAYS

"And then he actually added some more back here. So he's letting you know. He's in kindergarten. He drew the pictures. He wrote the words, and he made a book just like Eric Carle made his book."

TEACHING SEEDS

Use language that shows the writer's actions and intentions.

The key to mentorship is to make the connection to professional authors often.

Many children may still be wondering if they can really make books all by themselves, so what they see can make all the difference. When you choose students' books to share, keep these points in mind:

TOPICS

Variety is important, and be sure to tap into children's "funds of knowledge" (Moll, et al. 1992) by keeping topics grounded in your students' everyday lives and interests.

DEVELOPMENT

All children need to see something that matches what they think they can do, so include a real range of both writing and drawing development. Honor students' books equally with your talk and reading.

STRUCTURE

List books (like *Roller Skating*) are often easier than story books for children who are first getting started. The structure helps them stay with one idea and simply write *about* something they know.

LANGUAGE

If you plan to read a book, look for clear, simple language so it doesn't seem out of reach.

ILLUSTRATIONS

The pictures in a book don't need to be expert (in fact, it's better if they're not), but they do need to show meaningful intention.

As long as you don't name *having an idea* as the first step in the process, you won't risk children's *not* getting started because they don't have an idea.

Just as the writers' meeting ends, one of Lisa's students announces that she is going to write about her family. Having an idea for her book shows a certain developmental sophistication. Lisa responds, "Perfect. I love it when people write about family, animals. My son likes to write adventure stories. But I think we need to just go try it." You may have wondered, "Why didn't Lisa ask the other children about their ideas?"

Here's why. On the first day, plenty of children will sit down and get started, moving their markers or crayons on the blank paper, but without any real intention toward a particular idea. You'll need to do lots of teaching in the coming weeks to help children have ideas and stay focused on them throughout their books, but remember: *They don't need this teaching to get started.* As long as you don't name *having an idea* as the first step in the process, you won't risk children's *not* getting started because they don't have an idea.

Day 1:
At Work and Share Time

After the writers' meeting, the children get some tools and they go out to work on their first books. As expected, their first attempts show a wide range of development in both drawing and writing. Some seem to just be scribbling, but they're *busy* scribbling, all on their own, and that's what Lisa is hoping for.

When the kitchen timer goes off, the class gathers for a time of reflection. Lisa has asked two children if she can share their books with the class: Heidi, who thought she didn't know how to write a book but has finished a book about snowmen, and Alyssa, who has made a good start on a book about birds.

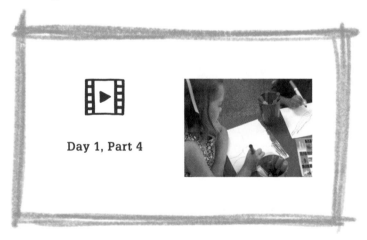

Day 1, Part 4

The typical range of development you might see

NOW CONSIDER

While students are out making their first books, you want to be right out there with them, observing them closely, taking notes on what you see, and most importantly, *responding* to them with joy and delight. Get to know your students as writers and illustrators.

You also want to be thinking very intentionally about whose work you want to share—and *why*—with the whole class during the reflection time. What you choose to share in the first few days of the workshop does important teaching and sets the tone for sharing and reflection for the whole year. As you think about who will share on this first day, consider the following questions:

QUESTION

How might I show a range of development in both drawing and writing?

TEACHING SEED

All bookmakers are valued here.

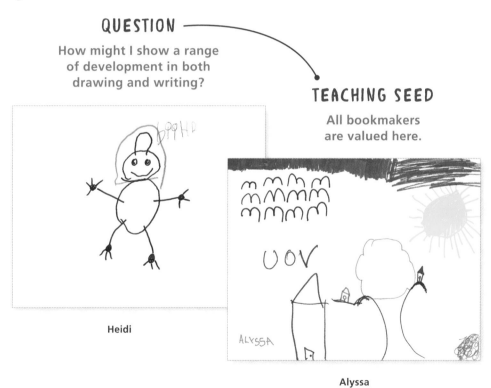

Heidi

Alyssa

Get to know your students as writers and illustrators.

QUESTION

How might I show process unfolding in different ways?

TEACHING SEED

It's okay to go about this in different ways.

Heidi

Alyssa

Heidi worked quickly and is "finished" and Alyssa worked much more slowly and carefully and only got two pages finished.

QUESTION

How might I lift the level of what other students are doing?

TEACHING SEED

We will learn from each other.

Heidi

Alyssa

Both Heidi and Alyssa had chosen a topic (snowmen and birds) and stayed with it across pages.

The writing process is not a set of steps to follow. The writing process is the story you tell after you write. Lisa is an expert at helping children tell stories of process. Here are some things to learn from the language she uses in the first share time:

Name the actions children took as they worked:

"Heidi sat down and started on this book, and she started writing right away."

Writing actions form the plot of a writing process story!

With thoughtful questions, lead children to name their actions:

"Did you draw all your snowmen on each page? And then you wrote on each page?"

Questions like these position children powerfully in their own narratives because they are the *only* ones who know the answers.

The writing process is the story you tell after you write.

Help children imagine how their stories of process might unfold over time:

"Tomorrow I'm going to hand your book back to you, and I bet tonight you will do some thinking about what else you're going to put in your book."

Like all good stories, stories of process need details:

"Heidi may think, 'You know, I think I can add more to that snowman book tomorrow. Like maybe my sister and I out there building that snowman."

Don't be afraid to be specific. Children need to hear models of thinking about possibilities.

In Your Own Classroom

As you plan for your own first day, keep the following two big ideas in mind. And remember, children will grow to understand these ideas with time and experience. The first day is just a getting-started day.

BIG IDEAS

Writing workshop is a time every day when you will make books.

People make books by drawing the pictures and writing the words.

TEACHING POSSIBILITIES

Compare to other *times* of day children already know (centers, lunch, recess).

Show children a picture of someone who is an author and illustrator alongside a book that person has made.

Show children books made by other children. Read one!

Show and talk about the tools you have available for making books.

Show children photographs of other children making books.

Use share time to talk about how children put words and pictures in their books.

NOTES

Day 2

NAME CHILDREN'S ACTIONS as PROCESS

The beauty of second days is that your students have done this thing called writing workshop before, and that changes the whole feeling in the room. It also changes how you plan for your teaching. You no longer have to rely on stories from other children to show what happens in writing workshop; the children sitting in front of you have stories to share now too.

Day 2:
The Writers' Meeting Begins

As the meeting begins, Lisa has the students' books from the day before in her lap. Her plan is to look at what they did and highlight all the different ways they went about making books. She also wants to help them think about how they'll work more on their books today. Lisa knows the "experienced" writers will lead the way when they go out to write, so she doesn't devote much time to talking about what will happen—even though five new children have joined the class.

The first book Lisa picks up is Alyssa's book about birds (which she'd shared the day before). When Lisa asks Alyssa if she is going to put writing in her book today, she says, "I don't know how," and then the meeting turns in that direction. Lisa invites other children who *did* put writing in their books to explain how they did it.

Day 2, Part 1

NOW CONSIDER

Let's think about questions for a moment. When you have a question, you generally ask someone you think would have an answer. Right? For example, who would you ask if you had these questions? Who would you never dream of asking?

> What's that funny noise my car is making every time I turn to the left?

> Where should we stay when we go to New Orleans?

> What can I substitute for molasses in this recipe?

On the flip side, have you ever been asked a question and you had no idea why? *Why does she think I have a favorite Prada store?*

Because they presume a certain identity, questions are powerful teaching tools. When Lisa asks Alyssa, "When you went home last night, did you think any more about this book?" Lisa is believing Alyssa into being the kind of writer who would have an answer to that question. When Lisa asks her a little later, "What do you think you're going to do?" she is teaching Alyssa that she is just the kind of writer who thinks ahead and makes plans.

The questions you ask your students teach them that you think they are *just the kinds of people* who would have answers. This teaching is particularly important at the beginning of the school year, because most of your students have probably never thought of themselves as the kinds of people who make books.

The questions you ask your students teach them that you think they are *just the kinds of people* who would have answers.

As you study the work your students do the first day, think about the questions you might ask that will help believe them into being the writers you want them to be. Be prepared—a lot of them won't have answers to these questions *yet*. But that's okay. It's the asking that matters.

A QUESTION LIKE THIS...
"This is so lovely. How did you decide which colors to use?"

SENDS A MESSAGE LIKE THIS...
You're a decider.

A QUESTION LIKE THIS...
"You have lots of letters here. How did you think of which ones to put?"

SENDS A MESSAGE LIKE THIS...
You're intentional.

A QUESTION LIKE THIS...
"You have your illustration here and your text here. Which did you do first?"

SENDS A MESSAGE LIKE THIS...
You have a process.

A QUESTION LIKE THIS...

"Have you ever written about flowers before?"

SENDS A MESSAGE LIKE THIS...

You have a history as a writer.

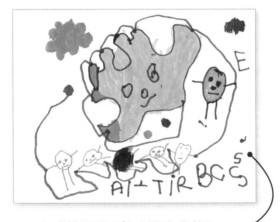

A QUESTION LIKE THIS...

"What do you think you're going to do next in your book?"

SENDS A MESSAGE LIKE THIS...

You're a planner.

Children are their own best teachers. While the explanations Alyssa's classmates give for how they put writing in their books may seem vague and not very helpful—"I just thinked!"—they are actually doing important work. Children who think they don't know how to write don't really need spelling lessons, at least not at first. They need to learn not to be afraid to try. The day before, when Heidi expressed this same doubt, Lisa didn't yet have any writers in the room who had met this challenge. On this second day she does, and that changes everything.

Tip

Some children will take longer than others to find the courage to try writing in their books. Be patient, remind them they can pretend, and keep nudging them to try. The won't learn to write if they don't try to write.

Day 2:
The Writers' Meeting Continues

As the meeting continues, Lisa returns to her original plan and tells how some of the children went about their bookmaking the day before. If you remember, Lisa didn't give the children any guidance about how to make their books because she wanted them to figure it out for themselves. Her job now is to name the actions she saw them taking—the writing process—and begin teaching them how to refine their actions over time.

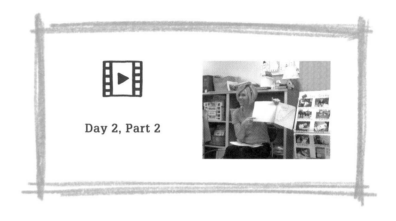

Day 2, Part 2

NOW CONSIDER

Everything that happens between an idea and a finished book is process. If your students are going to own that process, then they need some idea of what it means to be finished. Over the year, your expectations for finished books can grow right along with your students, but at the beginning, it's best to start simply. Lisa's beginning expectation is that children will make their best attempts at putting some drawing and some writing on every page of their books—what she calls "pictures and words."

> **Everything that happens between an idea and a finished book is process.**

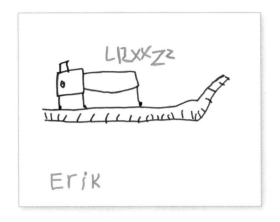

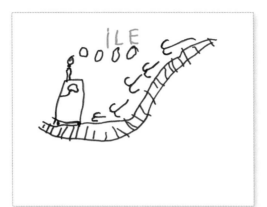

The first day, Erik made a book about trains, and he put pictures and words on every page. Lisa uses his book to help the other children think about a very important idea: What does it mean to be finished with a book? Here are some take-aways from her talk:

Emphasize "the look" of a finished book.

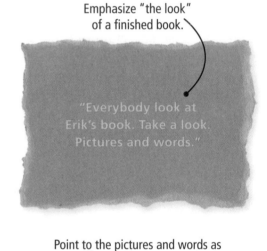

"Everybody look at Erik's book. Take a look. Pictures and words."

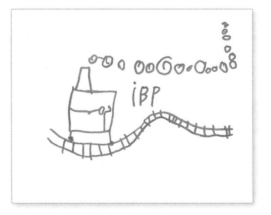

Point to the pictures and words as you talk about them. Not every child will be sure of the difference.

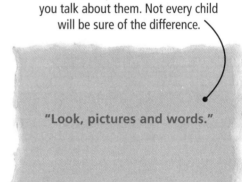

"Look, pictures and words."

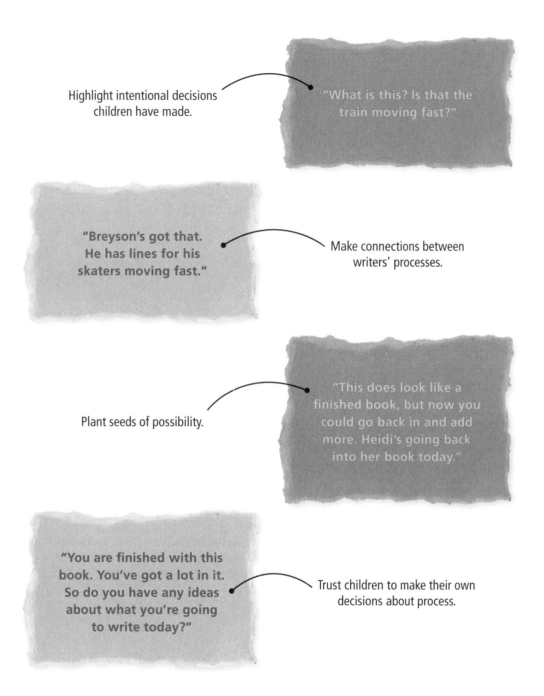

Highlight intentional decisions children have made.

"What is this? Is that the train moving fast?"

"Breyson's got that. He has lines for his skaters moving fast."

Make connections between writers' processes.

Plant seeds of possibility.

"This does look like a finished book, but now you could go back in and add more. Heidi's going back into her book today."

"You are finished with this book. You've got a lot in it. So do you have any ideas about what you're going to write today?"

Trust children to make their own decisions about process.

Many beginning writers have never really worked on a project over time. Help your students imagine how they can "go back in" to their books and develop them, and while you're at it, make this sound like a really fun thing to do: "You know, it would be so cool if this dragon had smoke and fire coming out of its mouth." Healthy attitudes about the recursive nature of process are built this way.

Tip

Returning to a writer's story (as Lisa did with Heidi and Alyssa) helps children understand how process unfolds over time.

Day 2:
The Writers' Meeting Concludes

To give the children one more image of *finished*, Lisa shares a book written and illustrated by a former student, Sam, who is the brother of one of this year's students. Choosing a book written by a sibling is a particular joy and is purposeful on so many levels beyond its author. Just like the *Roller Skating* book she shared the first day, the book has clear, intentional illustrations. The topic is from a writer's everyday life, and the structure of the book is a list book. And once again, Lisa uses her read-aloud voice to communicate so much about the sound of good writing and how she honors children as authors.

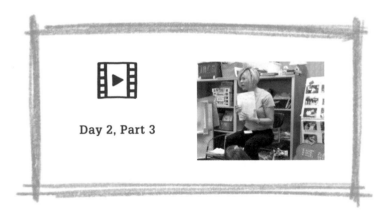

Day 2, Part 3

NOW CONSIDER

Teachers who devote a significant amount of time each day to writing workshop know that children are also growing as readers as they make books. As Lisa shares Sam's book, she capitalizes on three opportunities to support children as readers. You will no doubt find these same opportunities in your own teaching.

Tip

Opportunities to teach about letters and sounds and how reading and writing work abound, of course. The key is not to overwhelm every reading experience with teaching.

❶ READING THE ILLUSTRATIONS.

Beginning writers need to make lots of meaning in their illustrations, and similarly, beginning readers need to read the illustrations to make meaning. On this page, Lisa shows the children how she reads the illustration. Addressing Sam's brother, she says, "And I don't know if this is you or Sam, but one of you is hiding behind this bush because I see your hair. Isn't that cool?" The key is to show children how there is always more meaning in the illustrations than just what is said with the words. Using illustrations, nudge your students to *add* meaning to their own books and *take* meaning from the books they read.

Sam's book *Me and My Brother Jacob*

❷ USING PICTURE CUES TO FIGURE OUT WORDS.

Children will need this familiar strategy again and again in writing workshop—even with their own books! Until their spellings become more conventional, they will sometimes have trouble remembering the words they've written. When Lisa can't quite figure out one of the words in Sam's book, she shows the children how she uses the first letter, *s*, and the illustration to think of a word that would make sense.

❸ MAKING LETTER-SOUND CONNECTIONS.

"*S* sounds like *ssss*, like *Sam*." Lisa also takes the opportunity to connect the sound with a familiar word.

Books like Sam's offer demonstrations close to the development of the children you are teaching, and risk-taking doesn't seem so risky when children see others like them have been successful. How *you* respond to children's approximations is key, however. Notice that Lisa made no judgments about the word she couldn't quite figure out in Sam's book.

> Using illustrations, nudge your students to *add* meaning to their own books and *take* meaning from the books they read.

Day 2:
At Work and Share Time

Just as she did before, instead of giving the new children instructions on how to make books, Lisa sends them off to figure this out on their own with only an image of a student's book guiding them. Of course, the new children have more than just an image—they will be surrounded by children who started making books the day before. They can watch and follow along.

For the share and reflection time, Lisa highlights the important process idea of what it means *not* to be finished. The three children whose work she talks about will all be coming back to their books tomorrow—Heidi for the third day in a row! Lisa wants to encourage children to work on their books over time, so she conveys her excitement about children who are doing that.

Day 2, Part 4

Tip

You may be wondering how to share students' books if there is nothing there to read. Just *share* them! Talk about what you see. Ask questions. Make connections. Eventually you can teach children to read their books using their illustrations, but until then, just *share* them.

NOW CONSIDER

Which of these two statements do you agree with *more*?

A. ❙ Children should work quickly and make lots of
   ❙ books so they get lots of experience moving
   ❙ through the process and writing lots of words.

B. ❙ Children should discover the process of
   ❙ writing in authentic ways so they see writing
   ❙ as something that evolves more slowly and
   ❙ involves lots of decision-making along the way.

It's not an easy question, is it? Of course, good writing takes time, but do beginning writers really benefit from spending a long time doing what beginning writers do? When you look at the cover of this child's book, you might wonder if it makes sense to celebrate her long work on this single page. "What is she learning from this?" you ask.

A first book cover

With your teaching, a writer who works a long time on a book:

develops the stamina and attention to stay with her work over time. Writers need stamina.	learns to separate herself from her work in time and space but to keep it close in her thinking. Writers get some of their best ideas when they step away from their work but keep thinking about it.	learns to return to her work and think about what meaning she was trying to make. Even the most experienced writers return to their work this way.	experiences how meaning evolves over time when she circles back, revises, and moves forward.

NAME THAT <- - - -

PROCESS!

During share time, Lisa says that everything Heidi has added to her snowmen book—scarves, buttons, snowflakes, sticks for arms and legs—has just made the book better and better. With this comment, she's defining the purpose of revision, but she's waited to name this purpose until *after* Heidi has revised.

When children revise because it's the next "step" in the process, they're revising procedurally. You want writers who revise (and plan and edit and reread . . .) *intellectually*—because they *thought* to do it. As you watch your students at work making books, be alert to the process you see unfolding all around you and get ready to name it.

Suppose you . . .

overhear a child saying, "I'm going to draw a bigger tree on this next page."

This child is planning what will come next.

watch a child go get a book about bats, look at the photos, and then return to his own book about animals.

This child is doing research.

see two children both drawing on the same castle in one child's book.

These children are collaborating.

see a child look at the cover of his book, realize he's left off his name and the date stamp, and then add them.

This child is editing.

watch a child look at what he drew the day before, then pick up a marker and add some color to the red feather in a bird's wing.

This child is revising.

hear a child ask his friend if he thinks the lion he's drawn looks mean.

This child is getting feedback.

overhear a child saying, "This is going to say BOO! really loud on this page."

This child is rehearsing.

overhear one child reading her book to a table of friends.

This child is publishing.

In Your Own Classroom

The beauty of day two of writing workshop is the rich pool of children's writing you have from the day before. As you plan for the day, spend some time looking at what children have done and thinking about what you might highlight in your teaching.

BIG IDEAS

People make books by drawing the pictures and writing the words.

Making books is a process that happens over time.

TEACHING POSSIBILITIES

Share examples of what children did the first day and ask them questions about how they did it (process). Model the language of process by naming their actions. Point out things you notice.

Read a finished book written by another child.

Ask children questions about what they plan to do *next* in their books.

As a whole class or in pairs, invite children to think with each other about what else they might do in their books.

As you observe children at work, look for those who are "going back in" to their books and invite them to share.

Day 3

SET EXPECTATIONS ----> FOR <---- PICTURES AND WORDS

Just as toddlers won't learn to talk if they don't first *try* to talk, children won't learn to write if they don't first *try* to write. As a matter of fact, inviting your students to think about how babies learn to talk is a great way to help them understand why they need to just start writing—even when they think they don't know how. Just as more experienced talkers celebrate baby talk and recognize it for what it is—*a start*—writing workshop is a place where children's first writing will be celebrated in all its glorious approximation.

But first you have to get them trying.

Day 3:
The Writers' Meeting Begins

On the third day of school, the last group of children join the class. Several of them were in a preschool class the year before where they made books, and of course they're joining classmates who've all started making their first books. Lisa knows she can "act as if" and the new children will follow along.

The big idea of today's meeting is that writers put words in their books. Lisa wants children to use whatever concepts of print and word making they have to write every day, so the expectation that a finished book has both pictures *and* words is key. She starts by showing the children a "Finished Book" chart (see pages 62–63) from the year before, but when she offers the word *text* as a writing-specific vocabulary alternative to *words*, a possibility opens up. The children are familiar with *text* in another, smartphone context, and they know it means making words.

Writing workshop is a place where children's first writing will be celebrated in all its glorious approximation.

Day 3, Part 1

NOW CONSIDER

Sometimes children know a lot about the alphabet, but word making itself is more of a mystery. They may not have tried to write words on their own. If you suspect your students are familiar with texting, consider using what they know about this process to help them understand word making.

TEXTING
the name of your dog

Choose the letters on your phone.

WRITING
the name of your dog

Draw the letters in your book.

When setting an expectation that children will have both pictures and words in their books, timing is critical. If you expect this too early, a fair number of children might think making books is out of their reach. You first have to convince your students that they are capable bookmakers. The good news is it usually doesn't take that long. This is only day three, but Lisa's students are in a really different place than they were when they started. Why? Because in the past two days, Lisa has

trusted children to figure out how to get started making books on their own.

celebrated and shared children's efforts across a wide range of development.

noticed and named the processes children are using to make books.

basically "acted as if" children are capable and doing exactly what they need to be doing to make books.

By the third day, Lisa's students are already acting like the bookmakers she believes them to be, and now it's time to start teaching into their work and raising the level of what each of them is able to do. Lisa knows a lot of children can do more than they've been willing to try so far, but they need some nudging to get started.

Day 3:
The Writers' Meeting Continues

Lisa decides to use her own book to introduce children to the process of adding words. She has strategically waited to teach with her own writing because she needed children to get started without following her lead. Now that they're engaged as bookmakers, she can use her writing with less risk that they will just copy what she does.

Lisa has started her book about her son Clay and the sports he likes to play by drawing a few of the illustrations. She first invites the children to look at the illustrations and think about what the book is *about*. Then she shows them how she adds a title and her name to the cover of the book.

Lisa's book cover

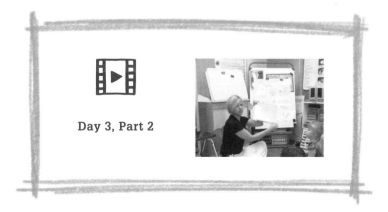

Day 3, Part 2

NOW CONSIDER

Take a moment to think about all the times during the day when you write in front of your students. Make a list here (it's okay, you can write in this book!):

1.

2.

3.

4.

5.

Anytime students see you writing, you can weave in talk about how written language works.

Anytime students see you writing, you can weave in talk about how written language works. All you need to do is narrate some of your actions as you write. The more mechanical aspects of writing are particularly well suited to teaching with talk like this:

Letter formation: "Watch me make this *K* . . . ."

Spaces between words and sentences: "I've written 'Today is' and before I write 'Monday,' I need to move over and leave some space."

Sweeping back at the ends of lines: "Here I am at the end of the paper, but I'm not finished with my sentence! Let me sweep down and back."

Punctuation: "I will put a question mark here because we're asking a question."

Capitalization: "I'm starting a new sentence, so let me use a capital letter."

Spelling strategies: "I'm going to picture the word *school* before I write it because I see it on the school sign every day when I come in the door."

In writing workshop, however, the writing you use in your teaching needs to match what you're asking students to do. If you just wanted to show your students how to think of letters to write words, you could use a whiteboard. But when children are making books, they're not just writing words, they're *composing* with words, and that's very different.

To compose, children have to . . .

THINK OF AN IDEA.

"This page is going to be about how my dog likes to play fetch."

THINK OF WORDS TO EXPRESS THE IDEA.

"Dallas loves to run and chase sticks and bring them back to me."

DECIDE WHICH WORDS TO WRITE.

"Whew, I think I'll just write, 'Dallas runs.'"

It's very big work.

The writing you use in your teaching needs to match what you're asking students to do.

Plan for a writers' meeting with one or two big ideas in mind, but also look for opportunities to embed teaching points in your authentic talk with children. For example, in the segment of the meeting you just watched, Lisa highlights

Books are about one idea.

Details are consistent across a book.

Illustrations tell you something about what a book is about.

A title tells you something about what a book is about.

Bookmakers think about the layout of illustrations and text.

Three lines of thinking will help you successfully embed big ideas in the talk of your teaching:

1
Have a solid understanding of what it is, exactly, children need to know about writing. You need to know this "by heart" because you can't plan ahead for most of this teaching. You respond with it in the moment.

2
Know what your students know. Look closely, listen carefully, and ask lots of questions about the books they are making.

3
When the moment is right, in kid-friendly language, embed big ideas you see your students need: "I like the way this tells you exactly how it happened." This statement conveys an important principle: *The ideas in a text should be organized in logical ways.*

BOOKSHELF

ALREADY READY
Katie Wood Ray and Matt Glover

The authors identify essential understandings about *all* writing and then show you how to look for them in *beginning* writing.

WHAT DO CHILDREN NEED TO KNOW ABOUT **TEXTS**?	TO FIND OUT WHAT STUDENTS KNOW, ASK YOURSELF . . .	IN KID-FRIENDLY LANGUAGE, EMBED BIG IDEAS.
Writers focus on a topic when they compose a text.	Is the child's book about something?	"Damon's book is all about his favorite thing—baseball."
The ideas in a text should be organized in logical ways.	How has the child organized this book? What is the connection between ideas?	"This is the perfect ending. I knew she was going to be happy when she got an ice cream."
The language in written texts has been crafted in particular ways.	When the child reads the book, does it sound like a book?	"Did you hear how she's written 'Oh my!' on every single page?"
Different publishing formats have particular features writers use to make meaning.	Is the child making the book *in the manner* of other picture books he's seen?	"He has a table of contents in this book, just like the dinosaur book we love so much!"
Different kinds of writing in the world serve different purposes for different audiences and have features in common that readers expect.	What does this book show the child understands about genre?	"I think Jody is the first to make a book that teaches the reader how to do something."
Writers use both illustrations (graphics and layout) and written text to make meaning.	How is the child representing meaning in this book?	"I can learn so many things about bats just from looking at Aiden's illustrations."

WHAT DO CHILDREN NEED TO KNOW ABOUT **PROCESS**?	TO FIND OUT WHAT STUDENTS KNOW, ASK YOURSELF . . .	IN KID-FRIENDLY LANGUAGE, EMBED BIG IDEAS.
Writers are purposeful and engage in a continuous process of decision-making as they compose a text.	Is the child intentional about what she is representing on the page?	"I watched Sara look back to match the colors of her outfit in her illustrations."
Writers make changes to clarify meaning, enhance style, make texts more readable, and so on.	Does the child engage in revision while composing the picture book?	"When he reread his book today, he drew a speech bubble around the words so you would know for sure that's what the clown is saying."
Writers think ahead as they compose, keeping the text as a whole in mind.	Is there any evidence the child is thinking ahead about what he'll write next?	"Trayvon told me in the bus line this morning what he is going to put in his book today."
Writers must stick to the task of writing to see a text through to completion (stamina).	How long has the child worked on this book? In one sitting? Over time?	"Heidi has been working on this book for four days now!"
Writers must be problem solvers.	Does the child exhibit a willingness to solve problems as he writes?	"Matt wasn't sure how to draw a monkey, so he went and found a photo online to look at as he draws."

WHAT DO CHILDREN NEED TO KNOW ABOUT BEING **WRITERS**?	TO FIND OUT WHAT STUDENTS KNOW, ASK YOURSELF ...	IN KID-FRIENDLY LANGUAGE, EMBED BIG IDEAS.
Writers choose topics that are meaningful (or find meaning in their assigned topics) and write for purposeful reasons.	How (and why) has the child decided to write this book?	"Izzy is making a book for her mother for her birthday."
Writing that is made public will be read, and writers are often mindful of potential readers as they compose.	How interested is the child in an audience's response to the book?	"I think the other kids are going to laugh when you read this to them!"
Writers often find aspects of composing to be very challenging.	Can I see in this book that the child has been willing to take compositional risks?	"AJ was sure he didn't know how to spell *nocturnal*, but he just gave it his best shot!"
Over time, writers come to know themselves in a particular way (as writers) based on their experiences.	As I interact with this child around this book, does it seem he has a sense of self as a writer? A sense of history?	"Martine has decided to write another book about Mexico. His third one!"
Writers are responsible for the words they put into the world.	Does the child show he understands his powerful position as author of this book?	"Martine is our Mexico expert!"

Day 3:
The Writers' Meeting Continues

After placing the title and author's name on the cover of the book, Lisa turns to the first full page. She's already drawn a picture of her son playing basketball, and the children help her decide to write the words *Clay is playing basketball.* On this first page, Lisa does most of the writing herself. She just wants to show what it looks like to add words to match the idea on an illustrated page.

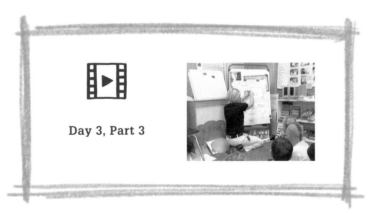

Day 3, Part 3

Every instance of writing in front of children is filled with teaching potential.

Again, every instance of writing in front of children is filled with teaching potential. The challenge is not to overdo your teaching. Take a moment to think about some of the things the simple text on this page offers that Lisa *could* highlight about word making.

Lisa's page about basketball

Every letter in the words has a name, formation and sound.

Play is just one letter different than *Clay*.

Other words can be made with *-ay*: *day, pay, lay, ray, may* . . .

The ending *-ing* is familiar.

Sometimes words aren't spelled the way they sound: /iz/ is spelled *is*.

Sometimes two words come together and make a compound word: *basketball*.

When you think about it that way, Lisa's demonstration is as significant for what it leaves out as for what it includes.

Here's an experiment for you to try that will help you understand something important about teaching beginning writers. In the space below, write a sentence that says something about the breakfast you had this morning.

Okay, so you just wrote a sentence and the experience of having written it is fresh in your mind. Answering a question or two about your process should be a breeze. What did you think about as you wrote the words? How did you know which letters to use to spell each one?

Tip

In writing workshop, always consider *why* you're modeling writing and what you want students to take away from the demonstration. This will help you stay focused and not overdo it.

Not so easy, is it? Most literate adults think very little about spelling as they write. The letters we need to make words come to us automatically. The exception, of course, is when we set out to write a word and we're unsure of its spelling or we know it's one that always trips us up. Then we become more strategic. We pay attention to how we're spelling—but only until we're past that word; then we're back on autopilot.

Well, when you're five, you're not sure of any of the words. Any of them can trip you up. Sometimes even your own name is a challenge when you're just getting started.

Here's the thing. As teachers of beginning writers, we can show children how we think of ideas, plan out pages in a book, or revise something to make it clearer, and the processes we demonstrate aren't that different from the ones children will use. But when it comes to showing children how to get words on paper, we're just not the same kinds of writers they are. We already know how to spell most everything we want to write, so we have to fake it and sometimes we offer sort of weird explanations for how we know how to spell, such as "I know how to spell *basketball* because I'm really pretty old."

BOOKSHELF

GNYS AT WRK
Glenda L. Bissex

Groundbreaking in its scope, an in-depth case study of one child learning to write and read.

AOF

AOELDMMO

Kolten

Day 3:
The Writers' Meeting Continues

One way to bring authenticity to a word-making demonstration is to invite children into the process, and that's exactly what Lisa does next. She asks for volunteers to come up and write the words as they continue adding text to her book about Clay.

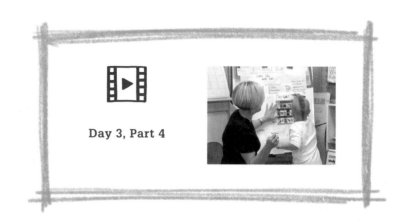

Day 3, Part 4

Adrian's baseball page

Lucas' scooter page

In a demonstration like this (designed to build confidence), children who know more about letters and sounds will sometimes correct an "off-the-wall" letter choice. If this happens, explain that you've asked the writer to put the letters he thinks should be there, and that different children may go about this in different ways.

NOW CONSIDER

Whether you're working with the whole class or one-on-one, helping beginning writers find the confidence to add words is teaching that has the potential to go off track quickly. Unfortunately, it doesn't take much to trigger an "I can't do this" response. How do you keep it *on* track?

1 Keep your goal firmly in mind: *I want children to use what they know to try and put words on every page.*

2 Remember that *what they know* is different for every child, and there is likely a wide range of knowing (and not knowing) in the room.

3 You won't know what they know unless they're trying to write, so you need to make this work!

FLAURS SMG

Let's look at a few of the things that happened and how Lisa used this line of thinking to keep the demonstration firmly on track.

When Adrian hesitates at the idea of writing a whole sentence, Lisa suggests she try one key word, *basketball*.

If a child seems to lose confidence, make the task more manageable to help her succeed.

After Adrian places a *B* on the page, Lisa asks her, "What else do you want to put?"

Think about how you're coaching the child's actions. "What else do you want to put?" gives the writer decision-making power, whereas "What comes next?" takes it away (it's already decided).

Adrian takes Lisa up on her offer to just stop with the letter *B* for *basketball*.

When you give a child a choice, honor the decision she makes, even if it's not the one you hoped for. This is how you build trust.

Lisa asks for another volunteer to write on the next page, someone who "thinks they would write more than just one letter."

Consider setting an expectation for what you want before you ask for a volunteer.

Lisa asks, "What would you write to put *scooter*?"

Remember, the goal for this demonstration is not to teach spelling strategies. That's why the question is framed this way and not "What do you hear in *scooter*?"

Lucas says he wants to put a *c* first for *scooter*. Then he sort of randomly picks an *h* as the second letter (perhaps because it is a familiar letter combination).

Again, remember that confidence is the goal of this demonstration, so you take whatever letter the child suggests.

For the final letter, Lisa invites the other children into the demonstration and asks them what sound they hear at the end of *scooter*.

Once a child is confident he can add letters on his own (you've achieved your goal), you might invite other children to help nudge the thinking a little.

Lisa ends the demonstration by reminding children that if they think they're going to have any problems adding words, they can use the alphabet charts and choose some letters from there.

Some children just don't have much letter-sound knowledge to work with at first, but it's still important for them to be writing in their books.

Day 3:
The Writers' Meeting Concludes

Just before the children go out to write, two girls who are new to the class announce their plans for the books they will make. Not surprisingly, their ideas for books are a lot like the one Lisa just demonstrated in her book, and they're enthusiastic because they know they "own" the names of their brothers and will be able to put these names in their books.

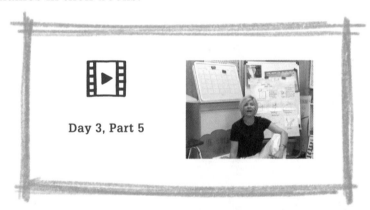

Day 3, Part 5

> **Bottom line, if children aren't trying to write, they're not learning to write.**

Asking children to write in their books when they don't know much about writing is a critical instructional decision. In many early-childhood classrooms, children are not asked to write on their own. Adults take dictation and do the writing for them. But dictation serves adults much better than children because most beginning writers can't read what adults write in their books. More importantly, though, as long as someone else is doing the writing, a child has no place to use what he's learning to grow and develop. Think about this: It won't be long before the child who wrote an *h* for the word *bird* learns that his buddy Breyson's name starts with a *B* and sounds a lot like the beginning of *bird*. As soon as he's got that, he needs somewhere to try it out.

Bottom line, if children aren't trying to write, they're not learning to write.

Day 3:
At Work and Share Time

Because of beginning-of-the-year technical difficulties with the lunch schedule (imagine that), there wasn't time for sharing and reflection on this day.

In Your Own Classroom

Every class is different, and some groups may not be ready for a nudge toward words this soon. If you feel like your students need a few more days to gain confidence, just continue sharing and talking about the books they're making. They will learn a lot from seeing what other children are doing. But as soon as you think they are ready, turn your attention to the "words" part of making books.

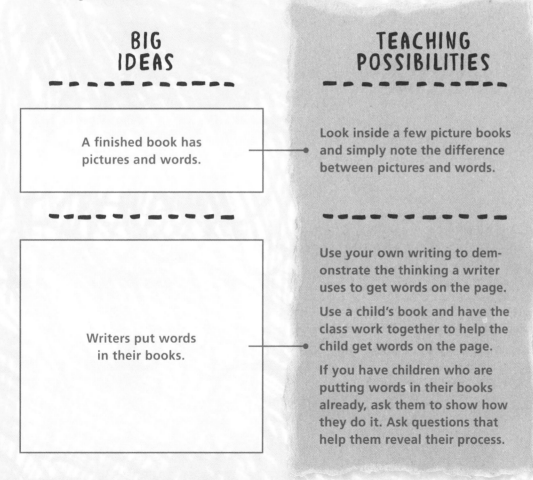

BIG IDEAS

A finished book has pictures and words.

Writers put words in their books.

TEACHING POSSIBILITIES

Look inside a few picture books and simply note the difference between pictures and words.

Use your own writing to demonstrate the thinking a writer uses to get words on the page.

Use a child's book and have the class work together to help the child get words on the page.

If you have children who are putting words in their books already, ask them to show how they do it. Ask questions that help them reveal their process.

NOTES

Is my book finished?

cover

1. Title
2. Date stamp
3. Fabulous illustration
4. Author and illustrator's name

inside the book...

Picture   words

text

illustration

Picture   words

text

illustration

Picture   words

SEES BOT

text

illustration

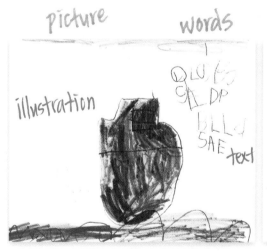

Picture   words

illustration

SAE text

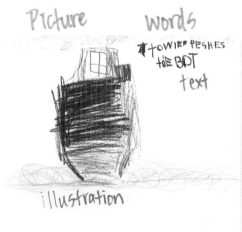

Picture   words

TOWIR PESHES tōE BOT

text

illustration

Picture   words

UBA text

illustration

Day 4

OFFER CHILDREN STRATEGIES ----> FOR WORD MAKING

As children begin adding words to the pictures in their books, you will no doubt see a typical range of writing (word-making) development:

Linear marks that sort of look like letters (mock letters)

Mock letters and random (actual) letters combined

Random strings of (actual) letters

Random strings of letters and visual memory (words they just know)

Invented phonetic spellings ("rainbow cat")

Children's first books show you what they are able to do on their own—to a certain extent. You may have children who know a lot about letters and sounds, but they've never been shown how to use that knowledge to spell because adults have always done the spelling for them. They know that words are supposed to be spelled in precise ways, and they're very aware they don't know how. Often, these children will use random strings of letters and sight words in their first books, but they will usually begin sounding out words with encouragement. Showing them *how* to strategically invent the spelling of a word builds confidence and helps them get started.

Day 4:
The Writers' Meeting Begins

Observing her students at work the day before, Lisa saw several adding words to their books, but they were more tentative than confident. In the writers' meeting that day, she mentioned lots of different ways writers decide which letters to put, but she didn't demonstrate this thinking directly because that wasn't her goal. Today, this is the goal, and her plan is to return to her book about Clay and have the children help her add more words to it. They start by rereading what they added to the book the day before.

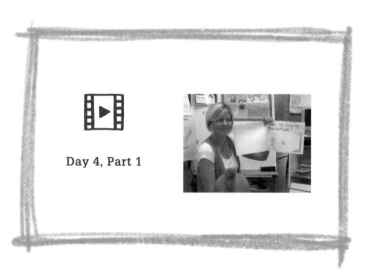

Day 4, Part 1

Think about how Lisa reads these pages of her book.

Clay is playing basketball.

Clay is playing baseball.

Clay is riding his scooter.

Without calling attention to it, Lisa reads these pages as if each contains a complete sentence. Only a *B* for *baseball*? No problem, especially when the picture so clearly shows a baseball and bat and helps the reader remember what the *B* is for. Not enough words to make an entire sentence? No problem, fill in the blanks and say the words that should be there. When in doubt, use whatever resources you've got to make it make sense. These are strategies children will need to read their own books once they start adding words.

Expand the definition of what it means to read—reading is more than word for word.

Tip

Save the books you use in demonstrations because you can return to them later in the year. For example, when her class studies illustrations, Lisa might pull out her book about Clay and revise the illustrations. When children already know about the books you're working on, you can move more quickly to whatever new thing it is you want to demonstrate.

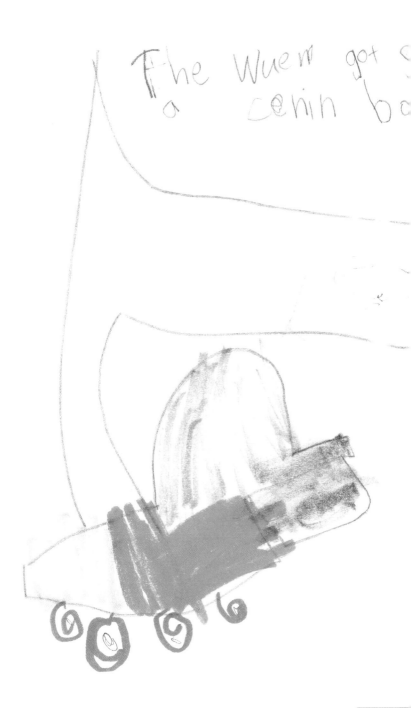

Day 4:
The Writers' Meeting Continues

Next, Lisa and the children set out to write "Clay likes to ride his bicycle" in her book, but almost immediately, Lisa decides to revise and substitute *bike* for *bicycle*. When faced with a choice of words, she chooses the one that best serves her purpose. The spelling of *bicycle* is much more complex than *bike*, and she wants to keep this simple.

Lisa's bike page

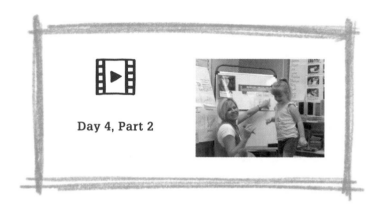

Day 4, Part 2

The pace of the demonstration is slower today as Lisa focuses more on the range of strategies children will need to put words on the page. She shows children how to say words slowly, isolate the sounds, use the alphabet card, and reread often for meaning. By the time she invites a child up to write the word *bike* on her own, Lisa has modeled how to sound out both *likes* and *ride*.

She also takes the opportunity to show the children that illustrations and text have to work together. Whichever comes first determines the other (or else the author must revise).

likes to ride
Clay ~~is riding~~ his bicycle.

Tip

In a demonstration designed to help children spell *strategically*, if a child offers an "off-the-wall" letter for a word, it's possible she's using some logic you're not seeing. Always ask before trying to steer her to a more strategic choice. And remember, a good strategic choice doesn't always lead to a conventional spelling.

NOW CONSIDER

When letter-sound knowledge is new, it's still tentative. Sometimes children will remember one aspect (the sound) and not another (how to draw the letter). And lots of times children need help finding the letter that makes a particular sound. This is where a good alphabet chart can be helpful.

At this developmental stage, most children who know letters know them in alphabetical order. If they need to see what a letter looks like, show them how to start at *A* on the chart and work their way to the letter they need. And if you have children who don't yet know much about letters, encourage them to use the alphabet charts to copy letters into their books. With your daily teaching about how language works supporting them, they'll soon be able to use the charts more strategically.

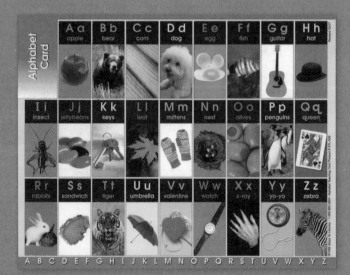

Chart courtesy of Steps to Literacy

We yoke et we
kad pye ysth
Lesx Tei sed
yes

For two days, Lisa has used the writers' meeting to show children how to put words in their books. She's highlighted multiple strategies and ways of thinking about this process. In the next few weeks, in both whole-class and one-on-one teaching, she'll circle back to these same strategies again and again with different words in different contexts.

You can use an alphabet chart and just choose some letters to make words.

Some words you just know how to write.

MOM   ME   LOVE

Think about whether you are writing a long word or a short word.

dinosaur   dog

Sometimes you can substitute one word for another word if it makes sense and seems easier.

television   TV

If you're thinking of a lot of words for your idea,

Dad is the fastest runner in the whole world!

you can just choose the main ones to write.

Dad runs fast!

Stop and reread what you're writing often so you keep the flow of your idea and don't forget it.

If you've already written a word once in your book, you can look back and use the same spelling again later.

 BOOKSHELF

YOU KAN RED THIS!
Sandra Wilde

Will help you understand more about how beginning writers develop understandings about spelling.

Sometimes you can picture a word if you think you've seen it before. What letters do you see?

school

At the beginning of each new day's work, reread your book so you remember what text you already have.

Most words have more than one letter in them.

bee you see

Think about initial sounds first.
What do you hear at the beginning of the word?

The sound you hear in one word—like a classmate's name—will sometimes match the sound you hear in another word.

Tristan tricky treat

Tip

For beginning writers, first focus only on the sounds you can hear in words. Once children get some experience sounding words out, then you can turn their attention to aspects of spelling that will help them remember silent letters, double consonants, and odd letter combinations like the *ch* in *school* or the *eo* in *people*.

Some letters actually make more than one sound, so you might have more than one letter possibility for the sound you hear.

circus city cake car

Say the word slowly and listen to each sound. Write the next sound you hear, then say it slowly again and write the next sound. Do this until you have all the sounds you hear.

Day 4:
The Writers' Meeting Concludes

Just before the children go out to write, Lisa pursues one more idea she believes will support a number of them in their work. You may remember that after day one, Heidi said she was finished with her snowmen book. But with Lisa's purposeful teaching, Heidi has become the poster child for stretching herself to do more than she first believed she could do. Today will be the fourth day she's worked on the same book. By highlighting this just as children are about to go write, Lisa sends them out with a sense of possibility, helping them see that writing truly is a recursive process rather than a linear march forward.

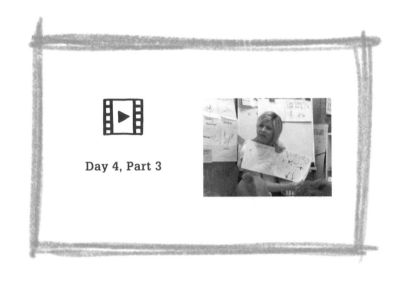

Day 4, Part 3

Every day children gain confidence by seeing how their teacher sees their work.

NOW CONSIDER

Think about how much of Lisa's teaching comes from looking at the books children are making and talking about what they have done. Every day children gain confidence by seeing how their teacher sees their work. When Lisa looks at Heidi's illustration of a snowman and says, "The arms are sticks, so they're brown," what she's really saying is, "I see you being intentional about the colors you're using."

Noticing and naming is really key to launching a successful writing workshop, and a lot of your work will involve observing your students carefully and finding things to highlight. Here's a getting-started list of the kinds of things you might notice, name, and talk about in children's work, knowing they will always surprise you with something you didn't expect to see.

When you look at the book your students are making, think about

the topics they are choosing.

what they're drawing in their illustrations.

how they're using color to make meaning.

how they're using all the white space inside their books.

how they're getting letters and words in their books.

the things they say about their work.

where they choose to work in the room.

how they use the tools.

how they are helping each other.

Day 4:
Share Time

At the beginning of share time, Lisa takes just a moment to address the noise level of the workshop. She knows that talk is essential for beginning writers. She doesn't want to silence the workshop, but she does want to manage the volume. She reminds the children that their talk should be about writing.

Next, Lisa turns everyone's attention to Madeline's finished book. Madeline had taken on the risky work of adding words to her book, and because this is something Lisa wants all the children doing, she decides to highlight it. Madeline's book is also a good example of adding one key word to each page (rather than a whole line of text), a demonstration that is developmentally right on target for many of her classmates.

Day 4, Part 4

Why do beginning writers need to talk during writing workshop? Because talk helps them

- grab hold of their thinking and develop it
- remember what they're writing about as they slowly generate text
- share ideas and possibilities for writing and illustrating
- sound out words and suggest letters to each other.

Teach the writer, not the writing.

NOW CONSIDER

One of the most important foundational ideas in workshop teaching is Lucy Calkins' (1994) sage advice to *teach the writer, not the writing.* If you remember this advice, it will influence your decision-making time and time again. But what does it mean, exactly? This share time is a perfect example. Madeline's finished book is a random collection of pictures and words. It's really not about anything. She and Lisa talked about this during the workshop, and Madeline now understands a book should be about one idea. But she'll take this understanding to her *next* book, because the point is not to make the writing better but to make the writer better.

But what about revision? What about editing? As children gain experience and confidence, you'll teach them strategies for both revision and editing, and they can use these strategies to make their writing better. The thing is, it doesn't matter *how much* better a single piece of writing gets as long as you can see the writer is learning and growing.

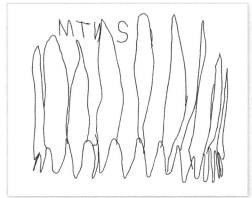
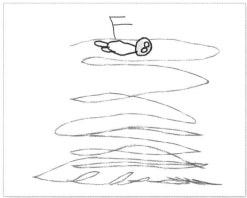

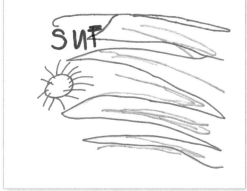

Madeline's finished book

EDITING POSSIBILITIES FOR BEGINNING WRITERS

You can help children develop a habit of going back and checking over writing, but just remember, a writer can't "fix" something if she doesn't know it needs to be fixed. What you teach children about editing needs to be developmentally appropriate. Start with just two or three guidelines like these and add others as children grow and develop during the year.

Check to be sure

your name is on your book.

you have a date stamp and a title.

you have pictures and words on every page.

your illustrations show lots of meaning.

your illustrations match your words.

you have enough information (in pictures and/or print) so you can read your book.

you have spaces between your words
(once a child has a sense of worded-ness).

you have enough letters in your words (long words should have lots of letters; short words should have just a few letters).

you have the best possible spelling, especially for words you read and write a lot.

you have used some punctuation in your piece (experimentation is fine).

Tip

During share time, focus on the stories of process you believe will most support your students. Some days those stories will be connected to the teaching in the writers' meeting; some days they won't.

Beginning writers are using almost everything they know to get writing on the page. Their writing looks the way it does *because they're five*, not because they're being sloppy or not trying hard enough. They're being brilliant, actually.

Their writing looks the way it does *because they're five*.

 BOOKSHELF

WRITING: TEACHERS AND CHILDREN AT WORK
Donald H. Graves

THE ART OF TEACHING WRITING
Lucy Calkins

All writing workshops—kindergarten through college—rest on the foundational ideas in these two books.

In Your Own Classroom

The big ideas for day four are almost exactly the same as they were for day three. The only difference is that the word *strategically* has been added. If your students need more time to gain confidence in just putting writing in their books, you might hold off on adding *strategically* to the mix for a few days.

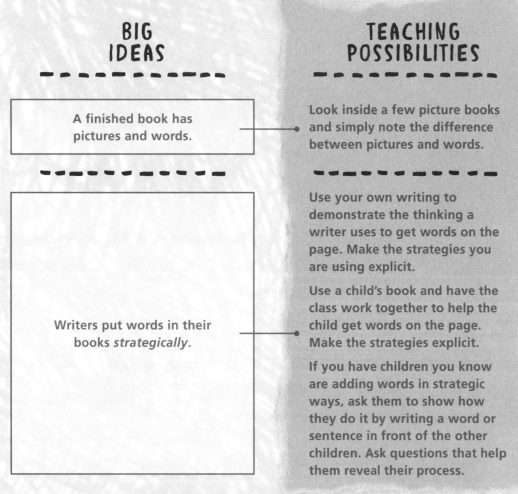

BIG IDEAS	TEACHING POSSIBILITIES
A finished book has pictures and words.	Look inside a few picture books and simply note the difference between pictures and words.
Writers put words in their books *strategically*.	Use your own writing to demonstrate the thinking a writer uses to get words on the page. Make the strategies you are using explicit.
	Use a child's book and have the class work together to help the child get words on the page. Make the strategies explicit.
	If you have children you know are adding words in strategic ways, ask them to show how they do it by writing a word or sentence in front of the other children. Ask questions that help them reveal their process.

NOTES

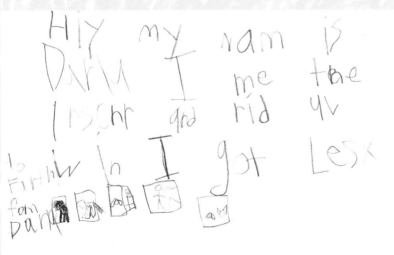

Hiy my nam is
Dahu I me the
Inschr god rid yu
to firithtr In I got Lesx
fom Dahu

Day 5

SHOW CHILDREN HOW TO MANAGE BOOK MAKING OVER TIME

Eventually, a weekend is going to come, and your very beginning writers are going to be away from their books for two whole days. Now that may not seem like a whole lot of time, but in truth, stepping in and out of work on a piece of writing is the central reality of every writer's life. Writers don't often finish drafts in one sitting. Writers have to go away and come back to their projects many times. And while writers have different routines for getting back into the work of writing, one strategy is essential to this process: *rereading*. Writers look back before they move forward.

Day 5:
The Writers' Meeting Begins

Because school started on a Tuesday, the fifth day of writing workshop falls on a Monday. Lisa knows the most important thing the children need to think about is how to get back into the work they started the week before. After all, there will be lots more Mondays to come, and days after holidays, and days after being out sick or on vacation.

Lisa's book about Clay

Lisa uses her book about her son Clay to show the children the thinking and actions she takes to reread what she has so far and then think about what she'll write next. She invites the children to "pretend I'm you" and imagine doing this same thinking with their books. Pretending this is easy. Lisa has a book she's been working on, just like they have. She has pictures and words in her book, just like they have. She's writing about something she knows about, just as she's encouraged them to do. And she's not finished yet, just as most of them are not finished.

Day 5, Part 1

NOW CONSIDER

Rereading, getting a sense of how a text is working as a whole before you add more to it, is arguably the most important process skill a writer needs. Writing well in small bursts is lovely, but writers have to make all those bursts work together effectively. The tool for that is rereading, again and again, and beginning writers are perfectly positioned to start using this tool. They may be rereading their illustrations, but teaching children to look back at what they have *so far* is both easy and also big, important work.

Naming what happens when writers reread will help you be more intentional in your teaching. When writers reread, they

remember exactly what the writing is about.

get the flow of the writing back—the tone, structure, and organization.

see the writing with new eyes, which leads to revision—of words, sentences, or whole sections.

edit for typos, format, and missed conventions.

consider what comes next in light of what's already there.

hear how the writing sounds inside a reader's head.

consider the thinking they've been doing (about the writing) while they were away from it.

Tip

Even children who have sounded out the words in their books are likely to need their illustrations to help them remember what the words are. Encourage them to use picture cues as they reread.

Pictures first or words first? Does it matter? It really doesn't. What matters is that each page has both, but children can decide which they will do first, pictures or words. The key is to teach them that whatever they do first leads the way. The text and the illustrations need to work together to make meaning. Some children will take more time to grow into this understanding, and you'll circle back to this idea often.

Day 5:
The Writers' Meeting Concludes

Rereading helps writers get started and move forward on a book they're working on, but moving forward also means deciding when you're finished and it's time to start a new book. For all kinds of management reasons, Lisa needs children to own this decision. So even though she doesn't yet have all the management in place that they need, she closes the meeting with some directions about what children should do when they think they are finished with a book (see pages 62–63). They take a quick look at the "Finished Book" chart, and then Lisa helps them picture the actions they'll take if they decide they are finished.

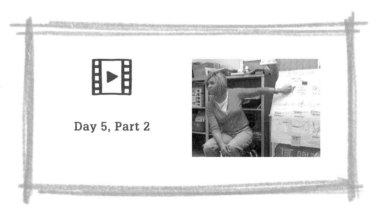

Day 5, Part 2

NOW CONSIDER

"Am I finished with this?" is perhaps the most elusive question every writer has to answer. If you went through it *one more time*, would you revise something? Find another edit that needs to be made? Decide to throw it away and start over? And being tired of working on something is not the same as being finished. *Finished* is a very difficult thing to know. For even the most experienced writers, "When is it due?" is a much easier question to answer.

> Spoiler alert: Five-year-olds don't really know that "Am I finished?" is a difficult thing to know. They happily decide they're finished without question or regret.

In the early days and weeks of the workshop, you have to act as if children will make good decisions about being finished. Now, as you might imagine, not every child actually makes good decisions. Some rush through books and put just a little on every page when they could do so much more. Others leave pages completely blank in their books. Some move on without putting words in their books; others forget to illustrate. Eventually, you will raise your expectations for the decision-making about being finished, but by letting the children own it right at the start, even when they don't own it well, you help them work independently in the workshop.

Day 5:
At Work and Share Time

During a long block of writing time, a few children decide they are finished. Tentatively, these children find partners and share their finished books. This routine will need a lot of support going forward as children learn to read their books, talk about their ideas, and listen and comment thoughtfully on each other's work. But for now they are approximating their best ideas of what this sharing should look like, and Lisa is fine with that.

For share time, Katie (who's researching in the room) shares the story of a conference she had with Erik in which she taught him how to read his book about vampires. As they were reading it together, they realized there was a page about a mouse that didn't really fit with the vampire idea. Katie explains how they revised their reading to make the mouse page fit with the others. Another good example of why writers need to reread.

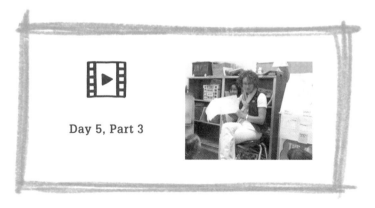

Day 5, Part 3

NOW CONSIDER

Learning to read their books so they sound like books (and not just point at the pictures and talk about them) is so important for beginning writers. Erik was writing with mostly random letters, but he wrote them confidently and seemed to understand the "pictures and words" requirement right from the start. When children are in this natural stage of writing development, reading their books is really a process of reading their illustrations. Some children will do this naturally, while others will need you to show them how. If a child says he can't read his book or he doesn't know how, here's the teaching process.

Here are the pages from Erik's book that show the movement from talking about it to reading it.

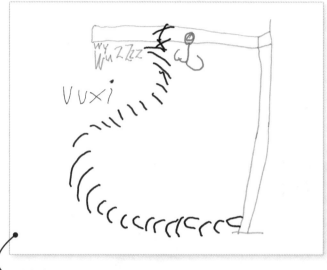

1 Have the child tell you about the illustration.

2 Ask any questions you have so you're clear on the meaning.

3 Take the central idea represented in the child's talk and craft some language for it that sounds like something you might read in a book.

4 Each time you add a new page, go back and read from the beginning so the child is hearing the reading multiple times.

ERIK: (Points to the figure at the top.) This is a mouse. And he runs all the way at the top.

KATIE: Do these marks show where he's running?

ERIK: Yes.

KATIE: Did he start running at the bottom?

ERIK: Yes.

KATIE: It looks like he's moving fast!

ERIK: (Nods yes.)

KATIE: Okay, let's read: *The mouse started at the bottom and went very fast all the way to the top until he broke through the top.*

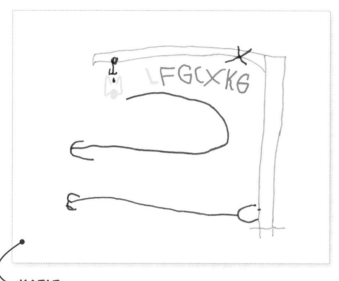

KATIE: (Noticing the same linear sides in the illustration.) Is this the same place?

ERIK: Yes. The vampire is flying around (pointing at the swooshing lines).

KATIE: Inside?

ERIK: Yes. He's looking for his family. But they're not there.

KATIE: Okay, let's read: *The mouse started at the bottom and went very fast all the way to the top until he broke through the top. / The vampire looked inside and he couldn't find his family.*

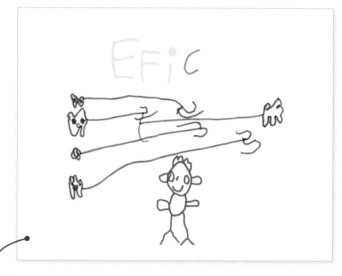

KATIE: Oh my, what's happening here?

ERIK: That's his family. These are the other vampires.

KATIE: He found them! He looks happy.

ERIK: Yes.

KATIE: Okay, let's read: *The mouse started at the bottom and went very fast all the way to the top until he broke through the top. / The vampire looked inside and he couldn't find his family. / The vampire found his family.*

BOOKSHELF

I AM READING
Kathy Collins and Matt Glover

This book will help you understand the kind of beginning reading Katie is teaching Erik to do.

ERIK: (Without prompting.) The vampires are back home.

KATIE: They look so happy. Okay, let's read: *The mouse started at the bottom and went very fast all the way to the top until he broke through the top. / The vampire looked inside and he couldn't find his family. / The vampire found his family. / The vampire and his family went back home.*

In the "Days After" chapter that follows this one, you can see another child, Abbie, read her own book to the class after doing this same work with Katie.

Tip

After several repeated readings, you might invite a child to read the book to you on his own. Don't worry if his reading doesn't match yours precisely. The goal is for him to do this kind of reading independently anyway.

At this stage of development, you can do all sorts of teaching about process with children's illustrations that will be much more challenging once they transition to having their words carry most of the meaning. Katie's revision lesson is a good example. Experienced writers often reread and realize either that something in a draft just doesn't seem to fit or that *how* it fits probably won't be clear to the reader (as it wasn't clear to Katie how the mouse fit).

When writers realize something doesn't fit, they are left with exactly the two decisions Katie suggests:

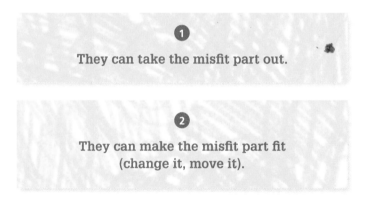

1

They can take the misfit part out.

2

They can make the misfit part fit (change it, move it).

Of course, knowing which to do is the hard part, but on this day Katie just names the revision dilemma and shows the children one of two options. And what's so great about revising when you're reading the pictures is that it's all very playful and easy. You can just say, "What if we read it like this instead?" and offer the child another way to think about how his reading might go.

Developmentally, the way a child reads a book will typically change a bit with each reading. The changes happen because most young children don't have enough conventional print to carry the message, so they must rely on illustrations and memory for each new reading.

When children reread their books in a different way, they are often making changes and adding details that make the books more interesting or easier to understand. Try not to pin down a child's exact meaning in a book too quickly; you don't want to miss out on these often richer readings.

Eventually, the meanings in students' books will become more consistent as their spellings become more accurate and children are able to hold the meanings more efficiently with words.

Tip

Tone matters. Whenever you talk about the need for revision, make sure there is nothing in your tone that suggests a writer has done something wrong.

Here are some descriptions of typical development
you will see as children are learning to keep their
meanings consistent.

*Illustration changes in
the moment.*

A child might start off
drawing a dinosaur and
change it to a dog halfway
through, and when it's
finished it's a picture of
a daddy. The illustration
literally changes as it's being
composed and continues to
change with each reading.

*The book is about the
same topic, but the main
details change.*

The child's book is always
about her family, but the
exact people or what the
family is doing changes
from reading to reading.

*The child reads the book
the same way each time on
the day it's composed, but
the words change on
subsequent days.*

This often happens as
words start to hold more
and more of the meaning,
but the spellings are still
very approximated. The
child forgets the logic of his
spelling approximations over
time and struggles to reread
and recapture his meaning.

*Meaning changes with
each reading.*

The meaning of the child's
book changes with each
reading. One time the book is
about a family, the next time
it's about playing outside,
and the next time it's about
something else.

*The book is about the same
topic, and the main details
stay the same.*

The child's book is about her
family doing the same thing
each time, though new details
may be added that enhance
the meaning and/or previous
details may be omitted.

*The child reads the book the
same way from day to day.*

This usually occurs when a
child has a lot of easy-to-
read spelling approximations
carrying the message.

From *Watch Katie and Matt . . . Sit Down and Teach Up* by Katie Wood Ray and Matt Glover

In Your Own Classroom

Most children don't just naturally know to look at what they already have before continuing work in a book. Until you teach this, you will almost certainly see children pick up a book in progress, find some open white space, and just start writing or drawing without even thinking about what the book is about. Sometimes, children who don't reread first are working on their books upside down and don't even realize it!

BIG IDEAS

A writer rereads before going forward with a book.

When a writer finishes a book, he starts another.

TEACHING POSSIBILITIES

Use your own writing and model the process and the thinking.

Use a child's book and coach him through the process as the other children watch.

Have children picture themselves finishing a book and starting a new one—talk them through it.

Show children a stack of books by one author (professional or child). Explain that being a writer means making lots of books over time.

NOTES

Let's Review the Big Ideas from the First Five Days

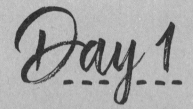

Day 1

INVITE CHILDREN TO GET STARTED

--> WRITING WORKSHOP IS A TIME EVERY DAY WHEN YOU WILL MAKE BOOKS.

--> PEOPLE MAKE BOOKS BY DRAWING THE PICTURES AND WRITING THE WORDS.

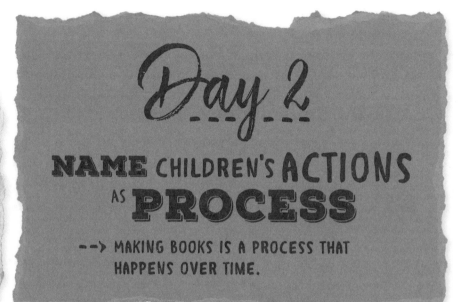

Day 2

NAME CHILDREN'S ACTIONS AS PROCESS

--> MAKING BOOKS IS A PROCESS THAT HAPPENS OVER TIME.

Day 3

SET EXPECTATIONS FOR PICTURES AND WORDS

--> A FINISHED BOOK HAS PICTURES AND WORDS.

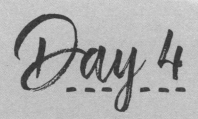

Day 4

OFFER CHILDREN STRATEGIES FOR WORD MAKING

--> WRITERS PUT WORDS IN THEIR BOOKS *STRATEGICALLY.*

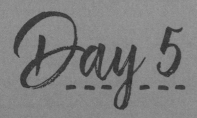

Day 5

SHOW CHILDREN HOW TO MANAGE BOOK MAKING OVER TIME

--> A WRITER REREADS BEFORE GOING FORWARD WITH A BOOK.

--> WHEN A WRITER FINISHES A BOOK, HE STARTS ANOTHER.

BOOKSHELF

READING, WRITING, AND TALK: INCLUSIVE TEACHING STRATEGIES FOR DIVERSE LEARNERS K–2
Marianna Souto-Manning and Jessica Martell

NO MORE CULTURALLY IRRELEVANT TEACHING
Marianna Souto-Manning, Carmen Lugo Llerena, Jessica Martell, Abigail Salas Maguire, Alicia Arce-Boardman

These two books speak powerfully to the need for culturally relevant (Ladson-Billings 1995) and culturally responsive (Gay 2010) teaching. They will help you think about how to communicate these big ideas specifically to the beginning writers in *your* care.

NOW CONSIDER

In your classroom, or in Lisa's classroom in a different year, this might not be the outline of the first *five* days of writing workshop. It might be ten days. Or seven. Or seventeen. What the story of this teaching reveals is not a daily lesson plan but an important progression of big ideas meant to help beginning writers get started making books. The ideas are recursive, meaning you'll circle back to them again and again throughout the year.

When you look at the five actions reflected in the chapter titles, don't forget how significant it is that expectations, strategies, and management don't come *first*.

When you recall the story of this teaching, consider how the following beliefs informed Lisa's every teaching move.

- Writing must be a predictable, daily *routine*.
- Children need to see themselves as writers, each with a unique *identity*.
- Writing is a process of *decision-making* and *action*.
- Writers need a disposition for *risk-taking*.
- Writers need a sense of *momentum* to know they are growing.
- Writers work with a sense of *craft* guiding them, and they learn craft from *mentors*.
- Teachers must *act as if* children are capable, competent writers.

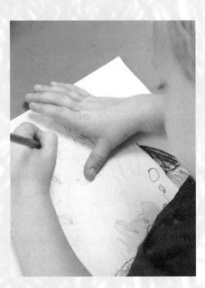

Days After

SUPPORT CHILDREN IN THE EARLY WEEKS OF SCHOOL

Your students will need all kinds of support in the first few weeks of school to keep their momentum going. In this final chapter, we've included six bonus clips of whole-class teaching from the first weeks of school in Lisa's class. Each one shows a different kind of support for beginning writers that is critical to the success of the workshop across the year.

Sharing Finished Books

As you saw with Erik's vampire book on day five, there is a process for teaching beginning writers to read their books. Since these books typically have few if any approximated (or conventional) words in them, you'll be showing children how to read the meaning in their illustrations and craft language that matches it. In the first few weeks, you'll do lots of this teaching in one-to-one conferences, and you will almost certainly see a range of reading development. For example, not all children will realize that the meaning should stay basically the same from one reading to the next. In other words, they do not yet understand that if these were vampires in your illustration yesterday, then they will still be vampires tomorrow.

To support a wide range of reading development, have children who understand this kind of reading share their books with the class. That's what Abbie is doing in this clip as she shares her book about her brother, Levi. In addition to her richly meaningful illustrations, Abbie has used a mix of random letters, sight words (friends' names), and the repeated sentence "I Love Levi" written on each page.

Writers Read Books

Abbie's book about Levi

NOW CONSIDER

Here are some important teaching moves to notice.
As Abbie shares, Lisa

names Abbie's "I Love Levi" sentence as a craft move, a *repeating line*. Abbie probably was just writing what she knows rather than crafting intentionally, but Lisa elevates the move by assigning intention to it.

reads the repeating line so it sounds like elegant word crafting.

compares Abbie's writing to Eric Carle's writing, helping Abbie see herself as being like this writing mentor.

explains that Abbie's book *sounds* finished. "Sounding finished" is an important new addition to the concept of "being finished" the class has been developing for days.

Encouraging Fearless Spelling

Beginning writers know and use many thousands of words when they speak and listen, but they recognize very few of these words in print. They don't need to shy away from these words as writers, however. As long as they have some beginning letter-sound knowledge to work with, they can invent a spelling for any word they know. The key is to help them not be afraid to try, and this too will take a lot of support in the first few weeks of school.

To celebrate and encourage risk-taking, Lisa uses an "I'm Not Afraid of My Words" chart to record children's fearless attempts at spelling. In this video clip, the class puts a word on the chart for the very first time. The clip begins just after Lisa has written Levi's spelling of the word *illustrator* on the chart: "LestorL."

Fearless Spelling

The most important thing to notice here is the distinction Lisa makes between children's approximated spellings and conventional spellings. She is very intentional about using the word *conventional* as she talks through the spelling of *illustrator*. Think about the message the words *right* or *correct* would send to children who are already timid about spelling. And in fact, *conventional* is the most accurate word, because spellings are conventions and they aren't set in stone. Sometimes they change over time, they can be different in different English-speaking countries, and the rules that govern them are sometimes arbitrary. Here are a few other teaching moves to notice in this clip. Lisa

— — — — — — — — — —

honors Levi's attempts and names the strategy he used by saying, "He *heard* a ____."

— — — — — — — — — —

doesn't try to explain all the spelling patterns in the word because that's not the point. The class can revisit the word later if she wants to talk about it more.

— — — — — — — — — —

draws attention to the length of the word, another important strategy for beginning writers.

— — — — — — — — — —

helps the children understand the developmental nature of approximation: "You're five!"

If you revisit a chart like this one, you can do all sorts of spelling inquiry that is grounded in words that interest your students. As you look at the conventional spellings, consider asking students questions like these:

> What letters are in this word?
>
> ILLUSTRATOR

> What other words do we know that are like this one?

> Are there any letter combinations you know from other words?

> Are there letters that don't make any sounds in the word?

> Is the meaning of the word related to its spelling in any way?

> Is there any mystery in the spelling of this word?

> Can we make other words from this word?

> Are there any endings or beginnings we might add to this word? Would they change the spelling at all?

Any talk you do about spelling should help children become brave, curious, and knowledgeable about words.

Any talk you do about spelling should help children become brave, curious, and knowledgeable about words.

Tip

If you encourage the use of dictionaries, word walls, and other spelling resources before children have become confident spelling without them, they may backfire. The message about correctness these resources communicate makes some children reluctant to try new words.

BOOKSHELF

PRESCHOOLERS AS AUTHORS
Deborah Wells Rowe

*CHILDREN, LANGUAGE,
AND LITERACY*
Celia Genishi and Anne Haas Dyson

*SOCIAL WORLDS OF CHILDREN
LEARNING TO WRITE IN AN URBAN
PRIMARY SCHOOL*
Anne Hass Dyson

These scholars document early literacy learning as a social process and can help you think about how to nurture a child's unique *self* among *others*.

Embracing Different Writers' Processes

The work you do in the first few days to notice and name children's actions as process will continue all year long and will teach children to think of themselves in particular ways ("I'm the kind of writer who . . ."). Strong identities build children's sense of agency as writers and help them grow with confidence. Because of this, you'll want to both create and take advantage of opportunities to talk about the different ways children go about their bookmaking.

In this clip, Lisa decides to have a conversation with her students about book titles. She's been using the word *title*, but the class hasn't really talked about what the word means or what titles do. As the talk unfolds, Lisa capitalizes on an opportunity to talk about how writers do things differently. One writer, Madison, has written a whole book and is deciding on her title after it's finished. Another writer, Alyssa, titled her book first and then started writing. A book has to have a title, but either process to decide on one will work, and each child needs to go with whatever works best.

Writers' Processes

NOW CONSIDER

This is another great example of how useful student writing can be as a teaching tool. With a folder filled with books made by other kindergarteners, Lisa

> makes the connection between what a book is about and its title. Many children may not realize there is a relationship between the two.

> uses other children's books to explore the idea of titles. Every time the children see other books made by kindergartners, they receive so many demonstrations of what's possible.

Lisa *took advantage* of an opportunity to talk about process in this teaching interaction, but you'll also want to *create* opportunities to talk about the different ways children are figuring out how to make their books. Consider talking with children about questions like these (each of them applies to illustrating as well as writing):

How do you get started each day in writing workshop? What do you do first?

Where do you get your ideas for writing?

Do you ever think about writing when it's not writing workshop time?

Where do you feel like you do your best work as a writer?

Do you draw first or write first?

Do you think about your whole book before you start, or do you think about it page by page?

How are our tools supporting you as a writer? Are there any other tools you need?

What do you think about as you reread your writing?

What is hard for you as a writer? What's easy?

What do you do when you get stuck on something in your writing?

Illustrating with Intention

Illustrators use pictures and writers use words, but they both *compose* meaning. The processes are parallel, and working with thoughtful intention in one medium supports thinking compositionally in the other. For beginning writers who still have a lot to learn about word making, composing thoughtfully with illustrations is the best way to engage with the process of meaning making—drafting, revising, and editing pictures that match their intentions.

In this clip of a share-time meeting, Katie highlights the work of two children, Will and Noah. Lisa's hope is that both boys will get a needed boost in confidence from having their work shared, but she also knows that drawing with intention is something she wants every child in the room thinking more about.

Illustrating with Intention

NOW CONSIDER

As Katie tells the stories of her conferences with the two boys, she very intentionally uses the word *compose* to talk about the process of drawing. She also

talks about the process in a narrative way, telling stories in which the boys are protagonists (Johnston 2004).

encourages the children to think about what things look like—colors, shapes—and match both their tools and drawing processes to what they see.

emphasizes the different strategies each child has used.

BOOKSHELF

TALKING, DRAWING, WRITING
Martha Horn and
Mary Ellen Giacobbe

This book offers smart, specific drawing techniques that immediately deepen the meaning making children are able to do in their books.

Supporting children's thinking about illustrations in writing workshop helps them

Build stamina for creative kinds of work and learn to stick with detailed tasks.	A child spends a very long time drawing bark on a tree in his book about hiking with his dad.
Develop habits of process: planning, designing, drafting, revising, and editing.	The child rereads and revises his drawing by adding a carving in the bark on the tree.
Utilize an important habit of mind: *how to read like a writer.*	The child notices how Marla Frazee draws individual blades of grass in her book *Stars* and then decides to add grass like this around his tree.
Learn about qualities of good writing in a parallel context.	The child's teacher comments on his powerful use of detail in the bark on his tree.

You can help your students compose their illustrations with more intention if you talk about illustrations in the picture books you read to them. Here's a list of a few helpful things to notice and discuss:

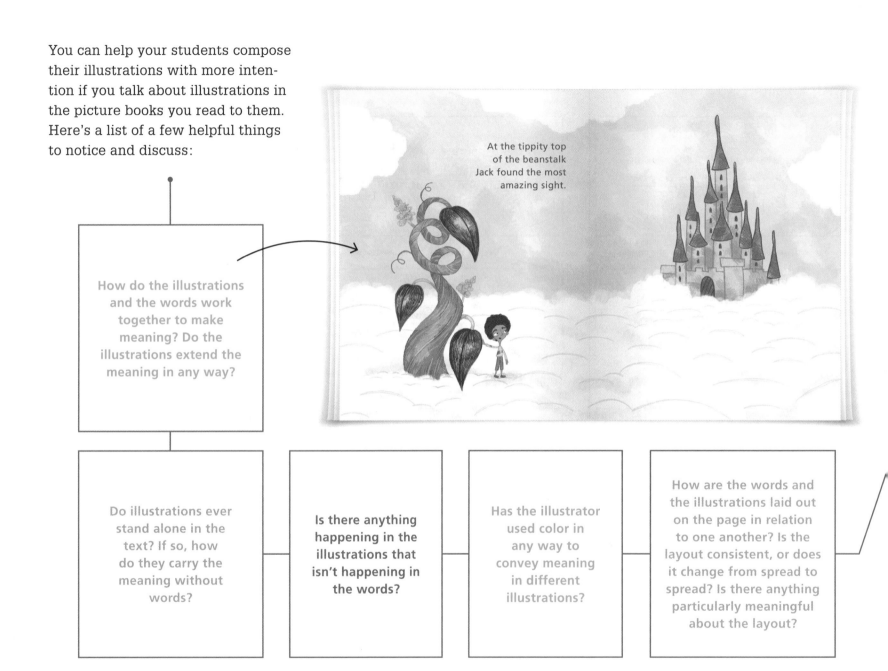

At the tippity top of the beanstalk Jack found the most amazing sight.

How do the illustrations and the words work together to make meaning? Do the illustrations extend the meaning in any way?

Do illustrations ever stand alone in the text? If so, how do they carry the meaning without words?

Is there anything happening in the illustrations that isn't happening in the words?

Has the illustrator used color in any way to convey meaning in different illustrations?

How are the words and the illustrations laid out on the page in relation to one another? Is the layout consistent, or does it change from spread to spread? Is there anything particularly meaningful about the layout?

Are there any words or print contained inside the illustrations themselves (signs, labels)?

What are the different angles and focuses (zoomed in and out) of the illustrations? Do these relate to the meaning in any way?

Is there any manipulation of the print (size, color, font, left-to-right orientation) that is meaningful in the text?

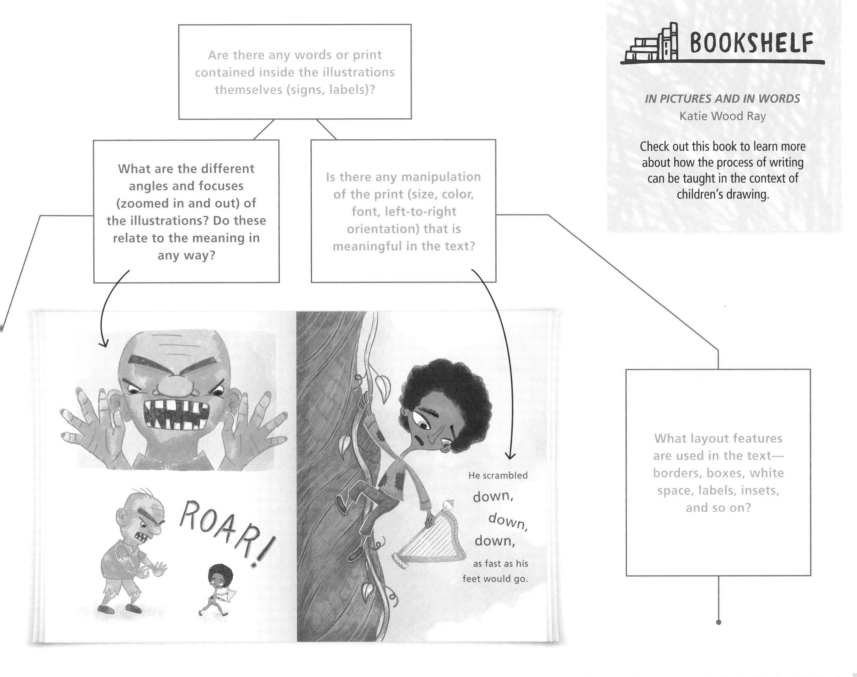

He scrambled

down,

down,

down,

as fast as his feet would go.

ROAR!

What layout features are used in the text—borders, boxes, white space, labels, insets, and so on?

Managing Ongoing Work

As you saw on day one, you don't want to overwhelm children with too many directions when you start, but you will need to introduce a few simple management routines for workshop over time. Routines, of course, help children work independently day after day.

In this clip, Lisa is showing the children how to use their writing folders. Up until this point, she has been taking their books up each day and handing them out the next, but she needs them to be able to do this on their own. She has the two boxes that will hold their folders beside her, and she shows the children exactly how to take their books in and out.

Management Routines

What's striking about the talk around the folders is how much is conveyed about *work in progress*. Writing is not an activity that begins and ends each day. Writing is a process that unfolds over time, and the folder routine is designed to help children understand it in that way. "The book you are *working on* always goes in front," Lisa says. As she explains the routine, Lisa

- - - - - - - - - -

makes a distinction between *finishing* and *finding a stopping place*. The difference is critical, and Lisa knows her language is critical too.

- - - - - - - - - -

explains the purpose of good management routines—they free her up to work with the children.

- - - - - - - - - -

As you think about what routines you will need to help children work independently, consider what it is they have to do *routinely*. Here are some questions to consider:

Where will you house your supplies? How will students get them and put them away each day?

Where will the books children are making be stored? How will they get them and put them away each day?

Where can children go to work in the room? Can they choose where they work? If so, what support can you give them to make good choices?

What should children do when they finish making a book?

How should children go about stopping their work at the end of writing workshop each day?

Are there any other routines you might need?

Celebrating Growth over Time

To build confidence and independence, children need to have a sense of momentum and to see that they are growing as writers all the time. You will need to be consistently on the lookout for signs of growth in children's work, and you will need to share and celebrate this growth often.

In this clip, Lisa devotes share time to celebrating work by Jaxon, a writer who has come a long way since the beginning of the year. As he stands beside her, Lisa shows the children Jaxon's first book, where he scribbled so hard on the paper that he made holes in it. Then, in a slow reveal, she shows them his current book about trucks.

Celebrating Growth

NOW CONSIDER

Notice how Lisa draws attention to the timeline of Jaxon's growth, pointing out the difference in his work from September to October. Highlighting time in this way helps children understand how their development happens *over time*, and it helps them trust that if they just keep doing what they're doing, they will grow. Lisa knows this, but it's important for the children to know it too. Here are some teaching moves to remember:

Lisa uses timely language, such as "This is Jaxon today." The unspoken message of this is that Jaxon tomorrow will be different, as will Jaxon next week, next month, and at the end of the year—all will be different as he grows.

Lisa shares Jaxon's first book, which is really just a scribbled mess, with no sense of judgment at all. She is letting the writing speak for itself, and she knows the contrast will be obvious.

When Jaxon says, "I wanted to write about tow trucks and dump trucks," he shows he understands that writing should be driven by intention, something that was completely missing in the first book.

One of the other children suggests, "You should put the sky." The children naturally think in compositional ways as they share each other's writing.

When the Camera Shuts Off . . .

Sometimes, what you don't catch on camera is the most important stuff of all.

After we'd taped this share session with Jaxon and turned the camera off, the children got up to stretch and move around a bit while we checked in with each other. As we talked, Lisa noticed it first. Jaxon was going around from classmate to classmate, giving out hugs. It was truly a beautiful thing to see. Abbie's comment that he had "really grown as a writer" seemed to have settled into Jaxon, and he just needed to continue to share the good feeling he had inside.

For both of us, that moment captured all our hopes for this work. All of them. First days matter so much because in the last days of the school year, when children sit and look at all the books they've made all year long, we hope each of them thinks just one thing:

----> "I'VE REALLY GROWN AS A WRITER" <----

And we hope this feels good to know, good enough to hug.

Bookshelf and Other Citations

Barnes, Douglas. 1992. *From Communication to Curriculum*, 2nd ed. Portsmouth, NH: Boynton Cook/Heinemann.

Bissex, Glenda L. 1980. *Gnys at Wrk: A Child Learns to Write and Read.* Cambridge, MA: Harvard University Press.

Calkins, Lucy. 1994. *The Art of Teaching Writing*, rev. ed. Portsmouth, NH: Heinemann.

Calkins, Lucy, Amanda Hartman, and Zoë White. 2005. *One to One: The Art of Conferring with Young Writers.* Portsmouth, NH: Heinemann.

Cazden, Courtney B. 2001. *Classroom Discourse: The Language of Teaching and Learning*, 2nd ed. Portsmouth, NH: Heinemann.

Cleaveland, Lisa. 2016. *More About the Authors: Authors and Illustrators Mentor Our Youngest Writers.* Portsmouth, NH: Heinemann.

Collins, Kathy, and Matt Glover. 2015. *I Am Reading: Nurturing Young Children's Meaning Making and Joyful Engagement with Any Book.* Portsmouth, NH: Heinemann.

Dyson, Anne Haas. 1993. *Social Worlds of Children Learning to Write in an Urban Primary School.* New York: Teachers College Press.

Gay, Geneva. 2010. *Culturally Responsive Teaching: Theory, Research, and Practice*, 2nd ed. New York: Teachers College Press.

Genishi, Celia, and Anne Haas Dyson. 2009. *Children, Language, and Literacy: Diverse Learners in Diverse Times.* New York: Teachers College Press.

Graves, Donald H. 1983. *Writing: Teachers and Children at Work.* Portsmouth, NH: Heinemann.

Halliday, M. A. K. 2013. *Halliday's Introduction to Functional Grammar*, 4th ed. Revised by Christian M. I. M. Matthiessen. New York: Routledge.

Harste, Jerry, Virginia Woodward, and Carolyn Burke. 1984. *Language Stories and Literacy Lessons*. Portsmouth, NH: Heinemann.

Horn, Martha, and Mary Ellen Giacobbe. 2007. *Talking, Drawing, Writing: Lessons for Our Youngest Writers*. Portland, ME: Stenhouse.

Johnston, Peter H. 2004. *Choice Words: How Our Language Affects Children's Learning*. Portland, ME: Stenhouse.

———. 2012. *Opening Minds: Using Language to Change Lives*. Portland, ME: Stenhouse.

Ladson-Billings, Gloria. 1995. "'But That's Just Good Teaching!' The Case for Culturally Relevant Pedagogy." *Theory into Practice* (34)3: 159–65.

Moll, Luis, Cathy Amanti, Deborah Neff, and Norma González. 1992. "Funds of Knowledge for Teaching: Using a Qualitative Approach to Connect Homes and Classrooms." *Theory into Practice* 32(2): 132–41.

Ray, Katie Wood. 2010. *In Pictures and in Words: Teaching the Qualities of Good Writing Through Illustration Study*. Portsmouth, NH: Heinemann.

Ray, Katie Wood, with Lisa Cleaveland. 2004. *About the Authors: Writing Workshop with Our Youngest Writers*. Portsmouth, NH: Heinemann.

Ray, Katie Wood, and Matt Glover. 2008. *Already Ready: Nurturing Writers in Preschool and Kindergarten*. Portsmouth, NH: Heinemann.

———. 2011. *Watch Katie and Matt . . . Sit Down and Teach Up: Two Master Teachers Reveal Their Thinking as They Confer with Beginning Writers*. Portsmouth, NH: Heinemann.

Rowe, Deborah Wells. 1994. *Preschoolers as Authors: Literacy Learning in the Social World of the Classroom*. Cresskill, NJ: Hampton Press.

Smith, Frank. 1988. *Joining the Literacy Club: Further Essays into Education*. Portsmouth, NH: Heinemann.

Souto-Manning, Marianna, and Jessica Martell. 2016. *Reading, Writing, and Talk: Inclusive Teaching Strategies for Diverse Learners K–2*. New York: Teachers College Press.

Souto-Manning, Marianna, Carmen Lugo Llerena, Jessica Martell, Abigail Salas Maguire, and Alicia Arce-Boardman. 2018. *No More Culturally Irrelevant Teaching*. Portsmouth, NH: Heinemann.

Strickland, Dorothy, and Lesley Mandel Morrow, eds. 1989. *Emerging Literacy: Young Children Learn to Read and Write*. Newark, DE: IRA.

Wilde, Sandra. 1992. *You Kan Red This! Spelling and Punctuation for Whole Language Classrooms*. Portsmouth, NH: Heinemann.

Vygotsky, L. S. 1978. *Mind in Society. The Development of Higher Psychological Processes*. Cambridge, MA: Harvard University Press.